How Can I HELP?

A TEACHER'S GUIDE TO EARLY CHILDHOOD BEHAVIORAL HEALTH

GINGER WELCH, PhD

Gryphon House

COPYRIGHT

© 2019 Ginger Welch

Published by Gryphon House, Inc.
P. O. Box 10, Lewisville, NC 27023
800.638.0928; 877.638.7576 [fax]

Visit us on the web at www.gryphonhouse.com.

LIBRARY OF CONGRESS CATALOGING-IN-PUBLICATION DATA

The cataloging-in-publication data is registered with the Library of Congress for ISBN 978-0-87659-833-7.

BULK PURCHASE

Gryphon House books are available for special premiums and sales promotions as well as for fund-raising use. Special editions or book excerpts also can be created to specifications. For details, call 800.638.0928.

DISCLAIMER

Gryphon House, Inc., cannot be held responsible for damage, mishap, or injury incurred during the use of or because of activities in this book. Appropriate and reasonable caution and adult supervision of children involved in activities and corresponding to the age and capability of each child involved are recommended at all times. Do not leave children unattended at any time. Observe safety and caution at all times.

CONTENTS

WELCOME

from the Author

Think back to when you made the decision to become a teacher. You likely had some idea about where you would be working, the sorts of children you would teach, and probably even some of the challenges you would face. Few teachers expect a huge financial windfall, but many of us expect emotional rewards for our sacrifices: the joy of seeing a child master a new concept, sweet thank-yous for drying tears and tending to boo-boos, and the sounds of little voices singing with you. I clearly remember building my expectations around a Norman Rockwell drawing of a teacher smiling before her class of unruly students, obviously touched by "happy birthday" messages scrawled on the chalkboard behind her. All misdeeds are clearly forgiven with their thoughtful gesture. Similarly, many of my fellow teachers "grew up" professionally with the expectation that the bad days that came with teaching would contain enough emotional reward to keep going. And truly, teachers who stay in the field must and do find these rewards.

However, many teachers—particularly new ones—have had the frustrating and puzzling experience of investing in a child and feeling that there is little to no return on that investment. Nowhere is this more apparent than in behavior management. When we treat children kindly, we do not expect a literal slap in the face. When we have modeled good social interactions, we do not expect to have strings of curse words spat at us. When we have established clear rules and created environments of consistent but warm guidance, we do not expect children to hurl chairs during group time. And when these things happen over and over again, we may begin to question ourselves, our competence, and our calling.

iv

How Can I Help? A Teacher's Guide to Early Childhood Behavioral Health

While quality teaching requires introspection about our abilities and our practices, many challenging behaviors in children arise because of difficulties in their lives that we cannot control. However, we can learn to understand and cope with these factors and consequently help children improve their behavior. This book provides a trauma-informed framework for working with children in the contexts in which they live, whether or not they have diagnosable disorders. This text can help you help the children who desperately need you to understand and nurture them in the busy early childhood classroom but who may not communicate those needs in a way that you can readily understand. Your classroom will always need the fundamentals of genuine care, respect, reliability, understanding, and compassion, and I hope you find useful ideas here for expanding those skills.

CHAPTER 1:

Three Lenses for Understanding Children's Mental Health

When we reflect on children's overall well-being, the popular term *mental health* can actually be a little misleading. We often think of skills such as coping, regulating emotions, paying attention, and relating to others as being solely part of mental health, but this perspective artificially restricts the connections between mind and body. In reality, mental and physical health are intertwined. An infant requires nurturing touch to grow. Cognitive techniques can assist patients in managing physical pain. Toxic stress—or severe, chronic stress without the benefit of a nurturing attachment figure— can lead to physical problems in the body. What we perceive as the separate domains of mental health and physical health are really one interrelated system of well-being, and developing a healthy child means paying attention to the whole child. To truly understand a child as a whole, it can be valuable for adults to conceptualize that child through three lenses: the biological, the environmental, and the relational.

THE BIOLOGICAL LENS

The biological lens focuses on the physical and genetic attributes of the child and invites us to look at elements such as these:

- Existing medical diagnoses
- Allergies

- Prenatal or birth history, such as prenatal drug or alcohol exposure or premature delivery

- Past problems with growth, such as failure to thrive

- Significant injuries

- Family medical history

- Any history of medical procedures or hospitalizations

Some of these factors, such as allergies, affect a caregiver's ability to keep a young child safe, so this information is usually collected at the time a child enrolls in a program. By remembering that mental and physical health are intertwined, however, we can see the need for even greater depth of information. For example, consider the following scenarios:

- Jackie has difficulty paying attention during teacher-led activities.

- Marco frequently argues with his peers.

- Seo-yun struggles to manage her emotions.

- Zion shows significant and unusual distress at drop-off time.

Adults often attribute problematic behaviors such as these to willful "acting out" that needs correction. Sometimes that is indeed the case. When we look beyond a behavior itself, however, we can often find biological factors that play significant roles in the situation. To continue the examples from before, consider this additional information:

- Jackie was born eight weeks preterm.

- Marco struggles with obesity.

- Seo-yun suffered a brain injury in a car accident when she was fourteen months old.

- Zion has a life-threatening peanut allergy.

As these examples show, the biological lens enables us to understand the potential contributions of a child's medical and physical status to her overall well-being. A child cannot control biological factors, but they affect her brain and body and therefore her behavior. This information, in turn, helps us better select our intervention strategies for challenging behaviors.

2

How Can I Help? A Teacher's Guide to Early Childhood Behavioral Health

Guidelines for Maintaining Privacy

The biological lens requires teachers to gather some medical information on children. How do we get this vital data while maintaining children's and families' privacy? Consider these guidelines.

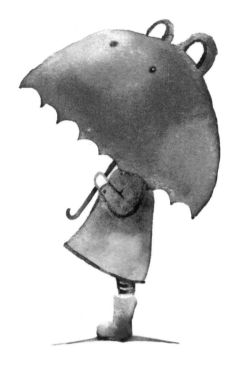

First, decide what information you need to gather for *all* children in your care. This includes two categories of medical data: general and individual. General information includes items such as a child's birth and developmental history, immunizations, and physician information. Individual information includes any medical details that you need to know to keep a specific child safe, such as allergies, physician-imposed limits on physical activity, current medications or therapies, problems with choking, and other medical diagnoses. Procedures for addressing such circumstances should be clearly listed in a child's records. You may also want to obtain information about family history for some disorders that have relatively high heritability rates (that is, they have strong genetic components), such as ADHD. Document both general and individual medical information in writing, and then double-check it in an interview with a family member during the enrollment process.

Second, decide how to gather each type of medical information. To obtain general medical information, you can have families fill out paper or electronic forms. You can gather most individual medical information in the same ways. However, some individual information may be particularly sensitive—such as prenatal drug or alcohol exposure, family mental-health history, or a history of abuse—so it may be better to discuss this information in personal conversations, as families are often unwilling to put such information in writing.

Finally, remember that building trust takes time. It is normal and prudent for people to withhold information that they consider private. (For instance, how would you feel if you took a class and on the first day were required to disclose the last time you drank alcohol, if you had ever used illegal drugs, or if you or a family member had ever had mental-health counseling?) Families may provide more information as they establish relationships with you. Sometimes they may initially deny that their child has any medical concerns but later disclose something significant. If this happens, you might feel upset about the deception, but resist the temptation to berate the family—you need to preserve their newly shown trust in you so that you and they can work together to meet the child's needs.

If a family member does disclose sensitive medical information about a child, how should you handle it? The following table includes some dos and don'ts for these conversations.

DO	DON'T
• ask family members for permission to discuss their child's health information with them. • offer family members unconditional positive regard.* • explain that all families are asked for this information, so no one is being singled out. • let families know why you are asking for this information. • tell families how you will keep their information private, and explain any exceptions to this policy. • protect children's records and limit access to them. • remember that it is reasonable for family members to feel anxious about disclosing information about their children's health. • respond to all communications about a child's health with respect and sensitivity.	• tell family members, "I'm sure none of this applies to you." This statement makes it harder for families to disclose information if there is indeed a concern. • share medical information with other families. It is unethical and undermines trust. • access information for children who are not in your direct care. • use slang or outdated, racist, or sexist terms. • act shocked or surprised by a family's disclosures.

*Note: According to Stephen Joseph of Psychology Today, *unconditional positive regard* is believing that a family is "doing their best to move forward in their lives constructively" and allowing them the freedom to choose how they do so. It does not mean that you have to condone the family's actions or ignore harmful behavior.

Overall, the biological lens helps us notice major factors that influence a child's behavior. However, biology does not determine everything about how a child will function and behave, and it certainly does not tell the child's whole story.

4

How Can I Help? A Teacher's Guide to Early Childhood Behavioral Health

Robin Parritz and Michael Troy summarize decades of research on behavioral genetics by stating, "All psychological traits show significant and substantial genetic influence. No traits are 100 percent heritable. Genetic impact is caused by many genes with small effects. Environments matter." In other words, even if a child has a genetic disorder coded in her DNA, she may not automatically display symptoms of that disorder. Genetic predisposition and environmental factors must both be present for symptoms to appear.

THE ENVIRONMENTAL LENS

Outside the field of early childhood, the term *environmental* might bring to mind images of conservation efforts, recycling, and a "green" world. However, if you ask an early childhood educator about a child's environment, she might tell you about the playground, the art center, and the child's family. More broadly, researchers Malin Eriksson, Mehdi Ghazinour, and Anne Hammarström define *environmental factors* in the early childhood context as everything in the physical and social realms that directly or indirectly touches a child's world. Here are some examples:

- The child's physical home
- School
- Parents, siblings, grandparents, and other family members
- Friends
- Family members' workplaces
- Economic well-being
- Government policies
- Religious institutions
- Social institutions

Groups of related environmental factors are called *systems*. Every child is nested within a series of systems. Urie Bronfenbrenner's ecological systems theory, described in his book *The Ecology of Human Development*, helps us understand children by examining how the systems affect the child and interact with each other:

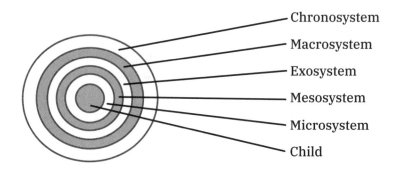

- **Microsystem:** At birth, a child is already the product of everything that affected her in the womb, such as nutrition, pollution, and stress. After birth and as she grows, she is influenced directly by all those who care for her, such as family members, child-care center or school staff members, physicians, members of religious groups, and friends. Together, all these influences make up her microsystem: the factors closest and most directly influential to her.

  » For example, married couple Esteban and Rafaella were in a serious car accident during Rafaella's pregnancy, so their daughter, Alejandra, was born prematurely and had trouble breathing for the first week of her life. Seven weeks later, Esteban and Rafaella placed Alejandra in a child-care center during the day so both parents could return to work. The environmental factors in Alejandra's microsystem include her parents, the car accident, her premature birth and early breathing problems, her medical providers, and her teachers at the child-care center.

- **Mesosystem:** The ways in which the elements in a child's microsystem relate to each other are also critically important. Those interactions—between home and school or between family members and friends, for example—create her mesosystem.

  » In Alejandra's case, Rafaella talks to her daughter's child-care providers each evening to hear about her day. She and Esteban also keep all of Alejandra's follow-up NICU appointments and write down information from her physicians. Both parents have good relationships with Alejandra's doctors and teachers and have signed a consent form so that the teachers and doctors can communicate about any medical limitations stemming from Alejandra's preterm birth. Rafaella and Esteban also find a great deal of support from

6

How Can I Help? A Teacher's Guide to Early Childhood Behavioral Health

the church they attend. In fact, church members often provide them with rides to medical appointments and occasionally babysit Alejandra. Alejandra's mesosystem is alive with helpful interactions.

- **Exosystem:** The exosystem contains relationships that may be direct for the child's caregivers but not necessarily for her. This level includes the relationships that the child's teachers have with her school, her family members' relationships with their workplaces and workplace policies, the quality of the neighborhood in which the child lives, and the influence of mass media or politics on all of a child's systems.

  » Alejandra's exosystem includes important influences from her parents' workplaces. Rafaella has poor job security and frequently worries about losing her job. Though she and Esteban would have liked to care for Alejandra full-time for longer, their companies' family-leave policies resulted in both of them returning to work when Alejandra was eight weeks old. These factors directly affect Rafaella and Esteban, but they have indirectly resulted in Alejandra's placement in child care and the distress she feels by sensing her parents' stress.

- **Macrosystem:** The macrosystem accounts for the influences of culture and historical context, such as major cultural or historical events.

  » Alejandra was born in the United States during a flu pandemic and a time of economic crisis in which many workers in her mother's field were laid off. Both of these factors are major sources of stress for her parents. Although all three family members are US citizens, Esteban and Rafaella also have increasing fears for their safety because of anti-immigrant sentiment. They identify strongly with their Costa Rican heritage and find strength in their church, prayer, and the support of extended family.

- **Chronosystem:** The chronosystem represents major events and points of transition or change across a child's lifetime. It shows the influence of time on all the other systems.

  » Esteban and Rafaella are married, but like many children, Alejandra may experience the significant disruption of her parents' divorce or remarriage during her lifetime.

Teachers and child-care providers function in the microsystem, the sphere nearest to the child, because they directly interact with the child as they care for her. However, the child exists within all levels of her ecological system at once and therefore is influenced by the factors within every level simultaneously. So, for example, not only is the relationship of the teacher to the child important, but so is the teacher's relationship with the child's family, her satisfaction at work, and her communication with her assistant teachers—because all these factors, in turn, directly or indirectly affect the child.

At birth, children are already involved in these complex systems. As they age and gain new experiences, their systems become even denser and more complicated. To support or treat a child's mental health, we must consider not just the child in isolation but also the influences from each level of her ecological system.

Teacher Task #1: Exploring Children's Ecological Systems

Think of three children in your care. Using the graphic on page 6 as a model, draw these children's ecological systems on a sheet of paper. Complete as much of each level as you can, paying close attention to where your influence comes into play.

On the back of your paper, answer these questions:

- What is your relationship like with each child, her family, and other providers in your organization? What about your relationships with other important people in the child's life?

- What ways can you brainstorm to strengthen these connections?

- Are there holes in your knowledge about a certain child's world?

- Are you developing hypotheses about how this child might experience the world based on her environments?

THE RELATIONAL LENS

Although Bronfenbrenner's model includes relationships, examining relationships separately from environmental factors allows us to focus on phenomena such as learning, family interactions and functioning, and met and unmet psychological needs. In his influential book *Childhood and Society*, psychologist Erik Erikson presents a theory of social and cognitive development that addresses many of these elements. This theory splits life into stages, each with a key task that a person must successfully complete to continue healthy development. If a person does not successfully accomplish a task, her future development and relationships are hindered by lingering challenges that stem from the failed task. This table (which also draws on the work of human-behavior expert Gail Gross) summarizes each task and the approximate age at which a person typically completes it.

8

How Can I Help? A Teacher's Guide to Early Childhood Behavioral Health

AGE (APPROXIMATE)	DEVELOPMENTAL TASK
Birth to 1 year	Basic trust vs. basic mistrust
2–3 years	Autonomy vs. shame and doubt
4–5 years	Initiative vs. guilt
6–11 years	Industry vs. inferiority
12–18 years	Identity vs. role confusion
Young adulthood	Intimacy vs. isolation
Middle age	Generativity vs. stagnation
Old age	Ego integrity vs. despair

The task of the first year or so of life is to develop trust and a sense of security. A child can do this only if she has reliable, nurturing, and responsive care provided by parents or parental figures. According to studies by Emma Adam, Megan Gunnar, and Akiko Tanaka and by Anne Murphy and her colleagues, these adults give care based on their own knowledge and capabilities, which directly correlate to the quality of the adults' attachments to their own parental figures. If those attachments were secure, they provide an appropriate model for caring for a child. For instance, DeAndre and Trinity both grew up in families with loving parents who acted quickly to meet their children's needs, so DeAndre and Trinity will probably follow those examples as they raise their son, Tyler. As a result, Tyler will likely learn that he can rely on others and be safe, both of which give him the confidence to explore and learn about the world as he grows.

On the other hand, if a child's parental figures had insecure attachments to their own parental figures, they may repeat harmful patterns because they do not know any other way of interacting with a child. For example, Rocky grew up with a physically abusive father, and Mindy's mother often left her alone for hours at a time. Rocky and Mindy love their son, Liam, and want to do better for him, but in difficult moments, they will probably fall back on the patterns they witnessed with their own parents. As a result, Liam might learn that other people are unpredictable and scary—after all, when he cries,

Mommy and Daddy sometimes cuddle him and sometimes slap him or leave him, and he does not know why. As he grows, Liam will constantly watch for danger (which, he knows, could appear at any time), leaving him with little attention or energy for learning.

As both of these examples illustrate, the foundations of a child's mental health are connected to her parental figures' mental health and functioning, as expressed in how they care for her. Furthermore, Erikson indicates that as the child ages and develops, the tasks that she must complete also change. Each success contributes to the child's overall well-being, while each failure can lead to new struggles now and later in life.

The relational lens, especially when combined with the environmental lens, helps us understand how a child's relationships—particularly with family members and caregivers—may affect her behavior.

· ·

For more information about children's development, consult the applicable sources in the "Resources" section from the Centers for Disease Control and Prevention, the Children's Hospital of Philadelphia, and Zero to Three.

· ·

WHY WE NEED ALL THREE LENSES

Children, along with their strengths and vulnerabilities, can appear in startlingly different ways depending on which lens we apply to them. It can be tempting to rely on a "favorite" explanation for behavior by primarily using a single lens (for example, "Charlie has ADHD. That must be why he constantly taps his pencil, frequently interrupts others, and never stays in his seat"). However, we benefit most from viewing a child through all three lenses, because then we can see a more complete picture of that child and her situation and can tailor our interactions accordingly.

For example, let's use each lens to examine a single behavior, such as self-stimulatory rocking in a toddler. Through the biological lens, we might see this action as a sign of autism spectrum disorder (see chapter 6). Through the relational lens, we might notice that the toddler has an older sibling who rocks—could that be where the toddler

10

How Can I Help? A Teacher's Guide to Early Childhood Behavioral Health

learned this behavior? Through a combined relational and environmental lens, we might notice that the toddler's family members always seem angry and disengaged from her care, so we may begin to suspect that the toddler's behavior originated from severe neglect and toxic stress. Not only do the three lenses point us to different possible origins of the behavior, but they point us toward different interventions. To find the best combinations of interventions, we need to look at each child in the contexts of her biology, environment, *and* relationships.

CHAPTER 2:

Foundational Tools for Promoting Mental Health and Well-Being as a Teacher

Obviously, you cannot control what happens to children outside of school. But as a teacher, you directly influence children's well-being through your relationship with each child and through the school or child-care environment that you share. So how, specifically, can you work to understand and address issues of mental health and well-being in young children? This chapter presents some basic tools that can help you regardless of what specific concerns you encounter in your classroom.

PREVENTION

When considering how to bolster children's mental health and well-being, it may help to view your role as primarily one of preventing problems. This prevention can be primary, secondary, or tertiary, depending on the situation and the needs of the people involved.

Primary Prevention

Primary prevention seeks to prevent family dysfunction or problematic symptoms from ever taking root in the first place and developing into mental-health issues. Primary prevention efforts are often implemented by professionals such as pediatricians, child-development specialists—and teachers. At this stage of prevention, we work to support and strengthen family members to raise physically and mentally healthy children. We build up protective factors around children and families to help them establish and maintain healthy functioning for a lifetime. The Center for the Study of Social Policy describes five protective factors that support children's development:

- **Children's social-emotional competence:** Building up these skills helps children develop socially and emotionally throughout life.

- **Family members' resilience:** Children benefit when their family members learn to cope, persevere, and overcome barriers.

- **Social connections:** Healthy social supports can provide needed socialization, modeling, respite, and comfort to families during times of stress.

- **Parenting knowledge:** Family members who understand typical development can respond to their children more appropriately than family members who misunderstand developmentally typical behaviors such as toileting struggles or picky eating.

- **Concrete supports:** Adults need access to the necessities of life to keep themselves and their children safe and healthy. Having appropriate food, shelter, education, and medical care is critical.

Teachers can help build up each of these protective factors. For example, teachers provide direct social-emotional nurturing for children. They help families connect socially through hosting program activities. Teachers can also provide opportunities for family members to learn parenting skills, such as information nights, and can help families connect to concrete supports that provide basic necessities, such as food banks, diaper banks, or free dental clinics.

Remember that even families who seem to function well can benefit from supports to maintain healthy functioning. Children and families do not need to have existing problems or diagnoses to receive assistance. Everyone, regardless of current functioning, can benefit from primary prevention.

For more information about protective factors, visit **https://cssp.org/our-work/ projects/protective-factors- framework**

Secondary Prevention

Secondary prevention focuses on helping children and families who already show symptoms of possible mental-health or family-functioning challenges and who may be at risk for developing additional or more severe problems. Secondary prevention seeks to manage symptoms and prevent the development of other mental-health problems.

14

How Can I Help? A Teacher's Guide to Early Childhood Behavioral Health

For example, a child with unusually active behavior may be diagnosed with a behavioral disorder if the adults around him jump to conclusions about the cause of his symptoms and immediately take him to his pediatrician to ask for medication. But before taking this step, a teacher could work with the child's family members to try an intervention to help manage the child's behavior. During this intervention, the teacher and family members may make careful observations and discover that the child acts restless because he misses a classmate who has moved away. In other words, this child is struggling with a relationship issue, not a behavioral issue.

Primary-prevention providers can still help families who are receiving secondary prevention services. Early intervention staff, who generally work with children in the earliest years of life, or infant-mental-health providers who focus on secondary prevention can also help families at this stage.

Tertiary Prevention

Some children may arrive in your classroom with existing mental-health diagnoses or with symptoms that meet the criteria for diagnoses. When we work with these children to relieve or remediate their symptoms and thus prevent future problems, we apply tertiary prevention. These children and their families must learn how to successfully cope with existing issues to improve their functioning and quality of life.

Children with mental-health diagnoses may work with primary- and secondary-prevention providers as well as with licensed counselors, psychologists, occupational therapists, or speech-language pathologists. These types of professionals generally only work with children to diagnose and treat specific disorders. Your role as a teacher in tertiary prevention may include implementing strategies from these professionals in your classroom, consulting with them, or informing them about how children function while in your care.

Teacher Task #2: Planning for Prevention

Are you beginning to get some ideas about ways you can provide opportunities for primary, secondary, and tertiary prevention to families at different times of the year? Try filling out each cell in the following table with your current ideas. After you finish this book, you may want to revisit this activity to see how your ideas have changed.

TYPE OF PREVENTION	BEGINNING OF YEAR	MIDDLE OF YEAR	END OF YEAR
Primary (supporting all families with ideas to promote healthy child development)			
Secondary (addressing risk factors and keeping early difficulties from worsening)			
Tertiary (managing current diagnoses and conditions to improve life)			

LEARNING THE LANGUAGE OF MENTAL HEALTH

As we saw earlier, looking at children through multiple lenses can help us find ways to educate, connect with, and nurture children in developmentally appropriate ways. However, to fully use these lenses to support children's mental health and well-being, we must also learn some of the terminology associated with treatment and intervention.

Diagnostic Sources and Terms

When a child (or an adult) is diagnosed with a psychological or behavioral disorder, that diagnosis most likely comes from the standard diagnostic system used by mental-health providers: the *Diagnostic and Statistical Manual of Mental Disorders*, fifth edition (hereafter the DSM-5). For each disorder, the manual provides an identifying number, a description of the disorder's symptoms and how they may develop, its prevalence, and the requirements for diagnosing it, such as tests that must be performed or how long symptoms must last to qualify as this disorder. Most disorders have additional specifiers that further narrow the description of a patient's symptoms. The DSM-5 is not a treatment manual and does not provide specific techniques for ameliorating a disorder. However, it is very useful for teachers to understand that mental-health diagnoses are not random: they come from a standardized source shared by counselors, psychologists, and psychiatrists. The DSM-5 can also help you, even if you are not a mental-health expert—for instance, if a child in your care receives a specific diagnosis, you can consult the DSM-5 to learn more.

A second source of diagnostic classification focuses specifically on infant and early childhood mental health. While the codes in *DC:0–5: Diagnostic Classification of Mental Health and Developmental Disorders of Infancy and Early Childhood* (hereafter *DC:0–5*) are not used for insurance purposes and are therefore less likely to be recorded by mental-health providers, they offer rich clinical information about diagnoses and conditions. The *DC:0–5* is not merely an early childhood version of the DSM-5; it provides significant additional information and revised categories for many of the most common infant and early childhood diagnoses and places additional emphasis on the developmental and relational contexts of young children. Early childhood educators may frequently encounter professionals, such as infant-mental-health specialists and child-development specialists, who rely on this manual to explain and understand disorders in young children. Along with the DSM-5, the *DC:0–5* is a legitimate source for learning about children's needs and behaviors.

Sensory Vocabulary

Many mental-health challenges, especially autism spectrum disorder (see chapter 6) cause children to have difficulties with their physical senses. Understanding sensory vocabulary will greatly assist you in learning more about specific disorders and in communicating with mental-health professionals about the children in your care:

- **Auditory:** hearing

- **Visual:** sight

- **Olfactory:** scent

- **Gustatory:** taste

- **Tactile:** touch

- **Proprioceptive:** body position

- **Vestibular:** balance and spatial organization

CASE STUDY:
DETERMINING
STELLA'S NEEDS

Use what you have learned about the lenses for mental health, the types of prevention, and the language of mental health to work through the following scenario.

Sixteen-month-old Stella will join your child-care program next month and will be placed in your classroom. Before your scheduled appointment to meet Stella's family, your director informs you that Stella was a preterm infant and spent eleven weeks in the neonatal intensive care unit (NICU) at the local children's hospital. Her twin sister passed away twenty-four hours after their birth. Because of alleged child maltreatment by her biological parents, Stella currently lives with a set of foster parents and their two sons, ages four and seven. Stella does not walk or smile and cannot feed herself. Her foster parents report that she has low muscle tone. She has regular appointments with the NICU follow-up team at the hospital where she was born.

Given this information, what are your hypotheses about Stella's needs at this time? What questions do you want to ask when you meet her foster family? Fill out these charts with your answers.

18

How Can I Help? A Teacher's Guide to Early Childhood Behavioral Health

BIOLOGICAL FACTORS	STELLA'S POSSIBLE NEEDS	QUESTIONS FOR FOSTER FAMILY
Genetic concerns or the diagnosis of a syndrome		
Health history		
Current health care		

Chapter 2: Foundational Tools for Promoting Mental Health and Well-Being as a Teacher

ENVIRONMENTAL FACTORS	STELLA'S POSSIBLE NEEDS	QUESTIONS FOR FOSTER FAMILY
Foster home		
Extended foster family		
Foster-parent employment		

RELATIONAL FACTORS	STELLA'S POSSIBLE NEEDS	QUESTIONS FOR FOSTER FAMILY
Relationship with biological parents		
Learned behaviors		
Interactions with foster family		
Interactions with biological family during visitation		
Early caregivers		
Parental separation		

Chapter 2: Foundational Tools for Promoting Mental Health and Well-Being as a Teacher

CHAPTER 3:

Trauma in Young Children

One of the most critical aspects of mental health and well-being for the children in your classroom is their personal trauma histories. We often think of trauma as involving horrifying yet relatively rare events, but this is not always the case. For example, Helen Egger and Adrian Angold studied a sample of American children ages two through five and found that, even within that narrow age range, up to 52.5 percent of the group had been exposed to trauma. In other words, more than half of those young children had suffered some kind of serious adversity. Because these types of experiences strike all demographic groups, there is an excellent chance that multiple children in your care each year will have experienced trauma. Thus, this chapter provides information on recognizing trauma and trauma-related disorders in young children, identifying trauma's effects on behavior, and setting up classroom supports for children who have been through trauma.

WHAT IS TRAUMA?

What exactly constitutes trauma? Colloquially, the term is used to describe everything from the end of one's favorite television series to a bad meal. This type of social overuse can lead to a general misunderstanding of true trauma and a serious underestimation of its effects on young children. *Trauma* is stress or harm (physical, psychological, or emotional) so severe that it disrupts the developmental tasks of early childhood, causing short-term or long-term problems. A child can suffer these effects from experiencing, witnessing, or feeling the threat of a traumatic event, whether once or multiple times. Here are some common experiences associated with trauma in young children:

- Physical abuse
- Sexual abuse
- Neglect
- Exposure to domestic violence
- Motor-vehicle collisions
- Loss of an attachment figure

Though not all children who experience traumatic events will develop diagnosable mental-health challenges, nearly all will experience at least temporary behavioral disruptions. Many children will experience long-term disruptions and will require formal interventions to help them change their behavior.

WHY IS TRAUMA SO DISRUPTIVE?

Children who have survived trauma have experienced the world as chaotic instead of predictable and as cruel instead of trustworthy. The assumptions necessary for these children to build healthy mental worlds have been violated, and this early chaos translates into behavior challenges. This happens through a significant chain reaction. According to a video titled "Toxic Stress Derails Healthy Development," available on the website of the Center on the Developing Child at Harvard University, the human body and brain respond to threats by releasing adrenaline, speeding up the heart rate, and elevating levels of stress hormones. When a child experiences severe, repeated stress—such as repeatedly witnessing violent interactions among family members—and does not have loving adults to help her manage her experiences, she remains in this aroused state all the time. As a result, the child's still-developing brain becomes overloaded with stress signals and makes fewer and weaker connections in the areas that manage reasoning and learning. In this way, trauma can literally rewire the brain for survival rather than for learning and healthy development.

For an excellent review of brain architecture, visit **https://developingchild.harvard.edu/ science/key-concepts/brain-architecture**

24

How Can I Help? A Teacher's Guide to Early Childhood Behavioral Health

Teacher Task #1: Your ACE Score

Traumatic events can take many forms, but certain negative childhood experiences tend to be linked with a significant increase in adult life problems, such as chronic illness, addiction, and early death. Visit **https://www.ncjfcj.org/sites/default/files/Finding%20 Your%20ACE%20Score.pdf** and complete the Adverse Childhood Experiences Scale (ACES) to find your own ACE score. Then, using what you know about the lives of the children in your care, try calculating the ACE scores for one or two of those children. While most people in the US have had at least one ACE, Vincent Felitti and his colleagues have found that an ACE score of 4 or higher is related to more-serious outcomes, including increased health problems and even early death. Additionally, Nadine Burke and her colleagues indicate that 51 percent of children with ACE scores of 4 or higher have learning and behavior problems in school, compared with only 3 percent of children with no identified ACEs.

POSSIBLE SYMPTOMS OF TRAUMA EXPOSURE

Some unusual behavior or functioning can have physical causes (for example, a child may cry at length because she has an ear infection), so encourage family members to consult their child's pediatrician as a first step. However, if no physical ailment can be found to explain the symptoms, the explanation could lie in the social-emotional or psychological realm.

Birth to Age Two

- Poor growth
- Developmental delays
- Problems with eating and digestion
- Problems with sleep
- Irritability
- Difficulty being soothed
- Aggressive behavior
- Withdrawn behavior
- Excessive fears
- Relationship difficulties with attachment figures
- Becoming particularly upset upon seeing people or objects that remind the child of the traumatizing event or events

Though children generally do not remember many specific details from the first two years of life, they can still demonstrate behavioral problems related to trauma that occurs during that time. In other words, infants and young children do not have to remember or be able to describe a traumatizing event to be significantly affected by it. For example, by around four months old, infants typically begin engaging socially by looking at others' faces, smiling, and showing pleasure. But an infant who has been ignored or responded to in a frightening manner may cease trying to interact when she sees a human face and instead withdraw or "shut down," such as by looking away or even falling asleep, according to the Raising Children Network.

To care for an infant who has been exposed to trauma, caregivers need to be trauma informed and acknowledge that the infant's challenging behaviors likely reflect her difficult early experiences. In general, the first interventions for challenging infant behaviors should focus on addressing the infant's needs (which we will discuss later in this chapter).

Over Age Two

- Symptoms similar to those of attention deficit hyperactivity disorder (ADHD) (see chapter 6)

- Overly active for age

- Trouble focusing on one thing at a time

- Impulsive behavior

- Trouble paying attention

- Poor relationships with adults and other children

- Difficulty being comforted

- Sleep, eating, or growth disruptions

- Imitating or acting out aspects of the traumatic event or events

Symptoms can seem contradictory at times, as some children will imitate the trauma they have suffered, while others may avoid all things associated with the trauma.

According to John Kihlstrom, professor emeritus of the Department of Psychology at the University of California, Berkeley, recovered memory therapy (a process that helps children "remember" what has happened to them) is a once-popular but now-discredited form of treatment for trauma. In fact, remembering is unnecessary for treatment, and this "therapy" harms rather helps.

26

How Can I Help? A Teacher's Guide to Early Childhood Behavioral Health

TRAUMA-RELATED DISORDERS

Children with histories of trauma may meet the criteria to be diagnosed with one or more trauma-related disorders. Some children may also meet the diagnostic criteria for other mental-health disorders, while other children will not meet the criteria for any diagnosis.

Here is a list of some trauma-related disorders from the DSM-5 that early childhood teachers commonly encounter:

- Reactive attachment disorder (RAD)

- Disinhibited social engagement disorder (DSED)

- Acute stress disorder

- Post-traumatic stress disorder (PTSD)

- Adjustment disorder

Let's examine each of these disorders more closely. The two primary sources of information on these disorders are the DSM-5 and the *DC:0–5*.

Reactive Attachment Disorder (RAD)

A child may meet the diagnostic criteria for reactive attachment disorder (RAD) if she has a history of serious neglect or if she experienced frequent changes in primary caregivers that precluded attachment in her first years of life. The criteria include these elements:

- The child is emotionally withdrawn or unresponsive, frequently in a negative mood, or unresponsive to or distressed by adults' efforts to comfort her.

- The child must have a social history (that is, a history of relationships and care) involving neglect or other attachment-prohibiting conditions, and this history must be responsible for the child's symptoms; they must not be accounted for by autism spectrum disorder (see chapter 6).

- The child must be at least nine months of age, and the problems must have existed prior to age five, as this is the period of time during which attachment forms.

What You May Notice

In the classroom, a child with RAD may have trouble socializing or responding to social efforts made by adults and other children. For instance, the child may not play with other children even if peer play is developmentally appropriate for her age, or she may show developmental delays in play. She may often seem to be irritable or in a negative mood, such as sad or angry. When she gets upset, she may be very difficult to calm.

What You Can Do

- Ensure that the child is safe and free from the neglectful conditions that resulted in the disorder. To do this, teachers must be diligent about recognizing and reporting suspected child maltreatment, including issues such as inappropriate caregivers, exposure to family violence, and neglect.

- Communicate daily with family members and other staff members about the child's functioning in your classroom.

- Respectfully ask the child's family members to obtain current, signed release-of-information forms and give copies to you to keep on file. These signed forms will enable you, the family, and other professionals involved in the child's care, such as child-protection officials, therapists, and the child's pediatrician, to share observations and ideas for supporting the child. (See chapter 7 for more about release-of-information forms.)

- Monitor the child for co-occurring developmental delays that may have also resulted from the child's history of neglect.

- Consistently provide responsive care, such as predictable nurturing and praise, even when the child does not reinforce your efforts. You may praise a child hundreds of times and find that she will still not believe that you love her. But at all costs, avoid giving up on the child.

- Minimize staffing changes in the child's classroom to ensure that a small set of familiar, loving adults regularly care for her.

- Children with RAD have generally experienced early chaos and unpredictable care. Follow clear, predictable daily routines that are also filled with nurturing interactions such as praise, hugs, recognition, attention, pats on the back, and patience. (These practices benefit all children, not just ones who have RAD.)

- Teach and use emotional vocabulary to help the child explain her feelings.

- Pay special attention to the child's interactions with her peers, offering supervision and coaching when needed.

Disinhibited Social Engagement Disorder (DSED)

Similar to RAD, disinhibited social engagement disorder (DSED) develops because of a history of severe neglect in which a child's emotional needs go unmet. These circumstances can occur because of a neglectful caregiver or an early life history in which the infant has multiple rotating caregivers. But while children with RAD have difficulty attaching to anyone, children with DSED fail to differentiate between familiar

28

How Can I Help? A Teacher's Guide to Early Childhood Behavioral Health

and unfamiliar adults when attempting to get their needs met. Children with DSED have been described as never having met a stranger—they behave as familiarly with adults they have just met as they behave with long-term caregivers. This behavior can endanger the child; for example, she might become friendly with an adult who has a history of child abuse, or she might be willing to follow a stranger out of a store.

What You May Notice

Children who are securely attached to their primary caregivers experience a few predictable periods of separation anxiety and stranger anxiety in the first two years of life. Most children exhibit their highest levels of confidence and security when they are near their primary caregivers, and they might become anxious or upset when they begin child care or school and are separated from these attachment figures. This phenomenon can be frustrating for adults, but it is part of typical development.

In contrast, a child with DSED might be overly affectionate with an adult whom she has just met. For example, a four-year-old with DSED might crawl into your lap as soon as she meets you, give you hugs and kisses, ask you to be her mommy or daddy, say "I love you" right away, or cross other physical boundaries. Note that an occurrence of one of these symptoms is not necessarily cause for alarm; in general, young children are affectionate, have poor understanding of physical boundaries, and frequently slip and call all caring adults "Mommy" or "Daddy" while at child care or school. However, if a child has a history of substantial neglect *and* shows a greater lack of caution with unfamiliar adults than is typical for a child of that age, these signs can be your first clue that the child might have DSED.

What You Can Do

- If the child has been removed from her home by Child Protective Services, ask the child's family members or guardians about the plan for establishing a permanent legal family for the child, if they have not already disclosed a plan.

- Communicate daily with family members and other staff about the child's functioning in your classroom.

- If the child is participating in therapy, respectfully ask her family members to obtain a current, signed release-of-information form and give a copy to you to keep on file. This signed form will enable you, the family, and the therapist to share observations and ideas for supporting the child. (See chapter 7 for more about release-of-information forms.) For example, if the child and the therapist are practicing appropriate physical contact, such as shaking hands with unfamiliar adults instead of offering hugs, you can reinforce the use of this strategy in the classroom.

- Include whole-class guidance about social-emotional topics such as appropriate boundaries (for example, being physically affectionate only with familiar people). Avoid singling out the child with DSED; instead, focus on teaching healthy behaviors to all children. This exercise can benefit all the children in your classroom. For example, have everyone practice shaking hands with a guest speaker.

- Provide all children with daily opportunities for working on social-emotional development, increasing emotional intelligence, and strengthening relationship-building skills. Pay particular attention to experiences about how people relate and the children's responses to these experiences. For example, ask the children what they notice about how a character in a book tries to make friends or handle feelings of rejection. Do the character's strategies work?

- Children with DSED need to learn that they can rely on trustworthy adults with whom they have relationships—they cannot rely on just any adult. Avoid guidance strategies that teach that all adults are powerful and that children should blindly follow them "just because." The concepts of authority figures and trustworthy adults are difficult for any child to grasp, but more so for a child with DSED.

Acute Stress Disorder and Post-Traumatic Stress Disorder (PTSD)

Many children experience or witness life-threatening or horrifying events. Some, such as a fatal car accident or a devastating earthquake, are one-time occurrences; others, such as arguments between family members, may recur and have a

> A traumatizing event that happens to a family member can also be traumatizing for a child.

cumulative impact. These children may have a wide variety of reactions, any of which can lead to a stress disorder. Acute stress disorder can be diagnosed almost immediately after a traumatizing event. If symptoms last one month or longer, a child may later be diagnosed with post-traumatic stress disorder (PTSD).

What You May Notice

All children experience and react to fear as a typical part of childhood. However, children with acute stress disorder or PTSD often appear to overreact to minor scares. For instance, if a classroom door slams unexpectedly, a typically developing child might startle, while a child with PTSD might run and hide under a table. These types of behaviors occur because children with acute stress disorder or PTSD demonstrate typical responses to atypical events; that is, their symptoms are understandable reactions for someone who has experienced something terrible. These children may have nightmares or seem to become numb to emotional experiences. They may

30

How Can I Help? A Teacher's Guide to Early Childhood Behavioral Health

experience apparent mood changes, such as increased irritability, sullenness, or depression. Their play may decrease or focus on reenactments of the traumatizing event. These children may seem jumpy and often have trouble with sleep, attention, and concentration. Some children talk frequently about traumatizing events, but other children avoid mentioning them altogether.

For an excellent review of childhood fear (both disordered and developmentally typical), visit **https://www.sbbh.pitt.edu/ Booklets%202113%20fall%20 2010/Fears_Matthews.pdf**

What You Can Do

Teachers play an important role in children's recovery from traumatizing events. Consider the following interventions:

- Encourage the child's family members not to wait to seek treatment for the child. If she is not already seeing a trauma-informed therapist, refer her to one. Respectfully ask the child's family members to obtain a current, signed release-of-information form and give a copy to you to keep on file. This signed form will enable you, the family, and the therapist to share observations and ideas for supporting the child. (See chapter 7 for more about referrals and release-of-information forms.)

- A child's trauma is a family's trauma. Recognize that trauma-related symptoms, such as behavioral and cognitive changes, may also appear in other members of the child's family.

- Communicate daily with family members and other staff members about the child's functioning in your classroom.

- Avoid "shutting down" the child. For instance, if a child tells you about a "loud, scary car crash," avoid telling her that "it will never happen again" or "everything will be okay now." You cannot keep these promises. Instead, try a response such as, "I heard about the crash. I'm so glad you're back in my class," or "It does sound like it was loud and scary. I'm glad that the doctors are helping you and your mommy." These messages acknowledge the child's feelings and experiences and also communicate that she is safe with you.

- Children often relive and process traumatizing events through play. For example, a child who was in a car crash might repeatedly ram toy cars together. Allow a child to engage in this helpful behavior, but be cautious about her expressing frightening or traumatizing details to other children. Observe play so that you can intervene if necessary.

Adjustment Disorder

Events do not have to meet the criteria for trauma to have a negative effect on a child. Sometimes a child has bigger-than-expected reactions to changes or stressful events, or these reactions may continue for longer than you had imagined. In either case, the child might be experiencing adjustment disorder. Symptoms include problems with anxiety, depression, behavior, or all three. They can appear soon after a stressor begins and may linger for up to six months after it has ended. These symptoms go beyond the expected adjustment period for a change in a child's life and are not part of the expected grief process. The DSM-5 ranks adjustment disorder as one of the most common trauma diagnoses, affecting up to 20 percent of people, including individuals across the lifespan and across cultures.

What You May Notice

Adjusting to change is difficult for nearly everyone, child or adult. People are drawn to predictability, even if change will bring something better. Many young children experience changes such as moving to a new home or school; losing a family member or gaining a new sibling; or even going on vacation. For young children, change can lead to developmentally appropriate but frustrating behaviors, such as crying, asking many questions, and experiencing disrupted sleeping, eating, or toileting patterns. However, a child with adjustment disorder will suffer much more intensely than a child who does not have the disorder and will experience symptoms for a much longer time.

For example, Carli's parents divorce, and her father receives custody of her. Carli moves into her father's new house and therefore transfers to your program. Her father always arrives punctually at pick-up time. But after four months, you notice that Carli still asks you every day, "Is Daddy coming to get me after school?" She also stays close to her female teachers, following them around the room and frequently demanding their attention. Every time it is Carli's turn to share during group time, she tells the same story about her mother not being able to see her, explaining, "She did something naughty, and the judge said I have to live with my daddy."

Carli's repetitive behaviors have become obnoxious to her teachers, who are now trying to either ignore her or prevent her from speaking during group time if she cannot talk about something other than her mother.

32

How Can I Help? A Teacher's Guide to Early Childhood Behavioral Health

What You Can Do

- If the child does not currently see a therapist, refer her to one. Respectfully ask the child's family members to obtain a current, signed release-of-information form and give a copy to you to keep on file. This signed form will enable you, the family, and the therapist to share observations and ideas for supporting the child. (See chapter 7 for more about referrals and release-of-information forms.)

- Communicate daily with family members and other staff members about the child's functioning in your classroom.

- Children often develop adjustment disorders after changes to their family systems. Communicate with the child's family members about changes in her life, including moving, divorce, remarriage, changes in health, deaths or other separations, or changes in the availability of family members.

- The child may talk to you about the stressor. Remember to respond with reassurance instead of with dismissal (for example, say, "You look happy when you talk about your dad," instead of "Well, that's all over now").

- Recognize that your school or program—and you—may be a stable factor in the child's life. Maintain a nurturing and predictable environment, and remember that sometimes the child will need extra help getting engaged in classroom activities. You can acknowledge her emotions ("You're thinking a lot about your mommy today") while also building bridges to help her engage in classroom activities with your social-emotional support ("Let's work on a picture together"). In this example, whether or not the child chooses to draw something related to her adjustment, she is getting the experience of being engaged with the class and feeling secure in her relationship with you, her teacher.

- Work on viewing adjustment disorder as the child's suffering, not yours. This disorder can indeed cause difficulties for you, but for the child, it means that her world or something in it has gone out of her control. Her anger, grief, and sadness (and the challenging behaviors that may result) are responses to help her make sense of what has happened.

- Avoid emotionally-punishing strategies. If a child has lost a parent, for example, never manipulate her by such coercive statements as, "What would your father think of how you're acting now?" These guilt-inducing techniques are neither motivating nor helpful, as noted in studies by Jo-Ann Donatelli, Jane Bybee, and Stephen Buka and by Aaron Rakow and his colleagues.

> The effects of trauma can last a lifetime.

- Anticipate social conflicts. Depression, anxiety, and behavior dysregulation in a child with adjustment disorder can cause peer-to-peer and child-to-adult conflict. Intervene early with calming strategies to help the child find a way to increase her sense of security and decrease conflict.

- When you intervene in social conflicts, respect the child's privacy. Avoid announcing to her peers that, for instance, she is upset because her parents have divorced. Instead, try placing a gentle hand on her shoulder and saying, "Let's take a few deep breaths together before we solve this conflict."

- Set up a quiet place in your classroom or building where a child can be supervised but have space to calm.

TRAUMA-INFORMED CARE AND GUIDANCE STRATEGIES

Children who have experienced trauma have experienced the world as unpredictable, frightening, or painful, and their behaviors may reflect their experiences. Additionally, as discussed earlier in this chapter and as noted by the National Scientific Council on the Developing Child, toxic stress can result in physical changes to a child's brain. Adults often tell children to calm down, but a child whose default brain state is alertness has great difficulty in complying with this instruction.

The next several sections provide strategies for caring for children who have experienced trauma. Note that while many of the basic ideas are suitable for all children, their specific applications vary to provide developmentally appropriate strategies for each age range.

> The Center on the Developing Child at Harvard University provides some excellent resources (including **https://developingchild.harvard.edu/ guide/a-guide-to-toxic-stress** and **https://developingchild.harvard.edu/ resources/inbrief-the-science-of-neglect-video**) on toxic stress and the developing brain.

Birth through Eighteen Months

During the first year or so of life, as Erik Erikson states, children's psychosocial task is learning trust versus mistrust. They need to learn that the world is trustworthy, predictable, nurturing, and reliable. Children who experience early life chaos and trauma may instead learn that the world is frightening, unpredictable, and painful. When you care for an infant or toddler who has experienced trauma, she is operating from this worldview. It will take more than a few days or weeks of your proving reliable and nurturing to undo this enduring belief! The following strategies, along with patience, can help you as you work with very young children who have trauma histories.

34

How Can I Help? A Teacher's Guide to Early Childhood Behavioral Health

BEHAVIOR	SAMPLE STRATEGIES
Excessive crying **Difficulty being soothed**	• Beginning at birth, respond immediately to crying in infants. • Always offer a label for emotions, such as, "You're feeling sad," even for preverbal infants. • Observe how the infant responds to cuddling, gentle rocking, patting, and other forms of physical comfort, as well as sounds and light. Some forms of sensory stimulation may agitate infants, while others may soothe them.
Developmental delays	• Meet the child where she is developmentally, regardless of her chronological age. • Provide the child with frequent exposure to excellent books and conversation. Avoid replacing interactive language with television or computer time. • Talk to your administrator about referring the child to a professional who can developmentally evaluate her. If you do make the referral, respectfully ask the child's family members to obtain a current, signed release-of-information form and give a copy to you to keep on file. This signed form will enable you, the family, and the professional to share observations and ideas for supporting the child. (See chapter 7 for more about referrals and release-of-information forms.)
Poor physical growth **Food issues related to possible early neglect**	• Feed young infants on demand. Avoid "pushing" them to begin eating solids or table food before recommended ages. • Children who have been neglected need to learn that food will always be available. Provide toddlers with reliable and regular snacks at frequent intervals, including a midmorning snack, an afternoon snack, and a bedtime snack. • Remind children of when the next meal or snack time will occur. Post schedules that they can understand, such as picture schedules, that include these times. • Children who have been neglected sometimes attempt to eat out of the trash. Ensure that your trash container can be securely closed.
Poor sleep quality	• Make sure that an infant is sleeping when she needs sleep and not on a prescribed schedule only. Infants do not have reliable sleep schedules until about six months of age, and as the American Academy of Pediatrics notes in "Study Suggests Parents Shouldn't Worry if Their Infant Doesn't Sleep through the Night by Six to Twelve Months of Age," families can benefit from additional information on typical infant sleep. • Watch for signs of sleepiness, such as yawning, fussiness, or gaze aversion. • Help the baby transition to sleep by soothing, holding, or rocking her.

BEHAVIOR	SAMPLE STRATEGIES
Lack of social interest **Withdrawal**	• Engage the infant in predictable and pleasurable games, such as peekaboo. • Reinforce any positive response from the baby, including when she pays attention to you, makes eye contact, squeals, or smiles. Your smiling face, gentle voice, and accurate responsiveness (that is, correctly identifying and meeting the need that the baby is communicating) will help her continue to engage. • Follow the baby's lead. Watch for opportunities to imitate her and create a game with her.
Excessive separation problems	• The strategies mentioned for clinginess can also help with separation problems. • Ask a family member to bring in one or more transition objects, such as a toy that brings the child comfort at home and may have a familiar scent or texture. For older infants, try laminating photos so that the child can touch or handle them.

Eighteen Months through Three Years

Between ages eighteen months and three years, according to Erik Erikson, children work on the task of autonomy versus shame. During this stage, children need to establish confidence that they can succeed at doing things for themselves without encountering excessive criticism or negativity. When children do not have the chance to successfully enjoy their own independence, they can internalize failure and struggle with self-esteem issues. Essentially, failure becomes part of these children, not just something that happens to them, so they think of themselves as failures and believe that they will fail no matter what they do.

Try these strategies to help toddlers who have experienced trauma.

36

How Can I Help? A Teacher's Guide to Early Childhood Behavioral Health

BEHAVIOR	SAMPLE STRATEGIES
Excessive crying **Difficulty being soothed**	Remember that children often experience developmental delays and behavioral regression in response to trauma. Provide the comfort and reassurance that the child needs, even if you deem it age-inappropriate.
Developmental delays	• Refer the child to a birth-to-three early intervention program, which you can find by searching "early intervention program [your state]" online. (See chapter 7 for more about referrals.) • Provide developmentally appropriate stimulation and comfort to the child. Consider the child's developmental needs and not merely her chronological age. The Centers for Disease Control and Prevention maintain a useful website (https://www.cdc.gov/ncbddd/actearly/milestones/index.html) that provides information on developmental needs.
Poor physical growth	• Refer the child to her pediatrician. Respectfully ask the child's family members to obtain a current, signed release-of-information form and give a copy to you to keep on file. This signed form will enable you, the family, and the pediatrician to share observations and ideas for supporting the child. (See chapter 7 for more about referrals and release-of-information forms.) • Observe the child's eating patterns and preferences, and note any unusual behaviors. • Model good eating by sitting at the table with the children and creating a peaceful atmosphere.
Poor sleep quality	• Ensure good sleep hygiene (see chapter 5). • Many children, especially those with trauma histories, have napping difficulties at "new" places, such as school or child care, so these situations require extra reassurance and patience from adults.
Aggression	• Model appropriate interactions for the child. • Use appropriate emotional vocabulary to connect the child's feelings with her actions. Model the way you want the child to respond to her emotions ("I think you're feeling frustrated and don't want to be around friends right now") rather than responding impatiently ("I've told you three times to stop hitting! Cut it out!"). • Practice brief (up to five minutes) structured and positive social interactions between a teacher and the child and between the child and one of her peers. For example, spend three to five minutes either working one-on-one with the child who is struggling or working with both this child and a more socially skilled child. During these periods, consciously model proper social interactions and how to express feelings appropriately through play. These experiences allow the child to practice discrete social skills, such as reading social cues, and allow you to model how to handle conflict.

BEHAVIOR	SAMPLE STRATEGIES
Lack of social interest **Withdrawal**	• Support the child where she is now; avoid forcing participation or excluding her from activities. Avoid statements that shame her or compare her to peers. • Communicate with the child's family to find out if her withdrawn behavior is limited to school. Respectfully ask whether she is receiving any therapy. • Allow the child to participate with you or with a highly skilled peer during social activities. • Teach the child to say, "Pass" in turn-taking activities. For example, a withdrawn child might still attend group time but not be willing to speak or share, so you can teach her to "pass" on these opportunities even while she still receives the benefits of sitting with her friends.
Clinginess **Excessive separation problems**	• Young children often do not know the words to express their feelings. Offer the child the words she needs: "You're so sad that Mommy's going to work today. She'll come back after outdoor time; we'll have fun until then." • Keep a single photo or a photo album of the child's family in a place where she can access it. • Provide or suggest that the child's family provide a transition or comfort item for her. • Maintain a predictable and posted schedule (picture schedules are great for young children) showing the sequence of the day. This helps all children understand the passage of time and when their family members will return. • Be patient with the child. Avoid a "toughen them up" approach. A child who clings to you is likely using you as a substitute family member for protection and nurturing, and verbal rejections such as, "Be a big girl," or "I'm everyone's teacher; you have to go play away from me" can cause further problems. • Reflect the child's feelings back to her and offer reassurance. If she says, "I miss Mommy," respond, "You do miss your mommy," offer a hand squeeze or a pat on the back, and say, "And I'm so glad that you're here with me today."
Sexual-behavior problems	• If the child is receiving therapy, respectfully ask her family members to obtain a current, signed release-of-information form and give a copy to you to keep on file. This signed form will enable you, the family, and the therapist to share observations and ideas for supporting the child. (See chapter 7 for more about release-of-information forms.) • Teach all children about appropriate physical boundaries, including rules regarding safe and unsafe touch.

38

How Can I Help? A Teacher's Guide to Early Childhood Behavioral Health

Three through Five Years

Preschoolers (children ages three through five) are more verbal than infants and toddlers. Though young children may be able to talk about traumatizing events, they most commonly express their experiences through play and behavior. Erik Erikson theorizes that children in this age range face the task of initiative versus guilt, so they need opportunities to initiate friendships, engage in meaningful activities, and successfully exercise control over themselves and their environments, such as by choosing what clothes to wear. If adults never allow a child to have control of something, punish her for demonstrating control, or excessively criticize her, she may become prone to putting herself down or acting out.

3—5 YEARS

BEHAVIOR	SAMPLE STRATEGIES
Excessive crying, anger, or problems with emotional regulation	Three-to-five-year-olds have strong emotions and are just learning the beginning steps of self-control. Adults must demonstrate the coping behaviors they want to see in children.
Learning problems	• Children with trauma often have trouble paying attention and can miss out on lessons. They may also struggle with memorization tasks. • Can you intersperse lessons with opportunities for movement and breaks? • Does the child show a difference when instructions are presented orally, with a picture, or both? • Does working with a partner help or hinder the child's performance? • What triggers do you notice that set the child off? • Make sure that the child has opportunities for movement and play; avoid taking away outdoor play or physical education as punishment for challenging behaviors. • Talk to your administrator about referring the child to a mental-health professional for an intellectual assessment.
Daytime sleepiness	• Ensure good sleep hygiene (see chapter 5). Children with trauma may experience disrupted sleep. • Communicate with the family about bedtime, whether the child has problems falling asleep, staying asleep, or both. Ask about whether the child snores, as this can be an indicator of poor sleep quality. • Ask the family to communicate with their pediatrician. • Look for signs of neglect or crisis, such as homelessness.

BEHAVIOR	SAMPLE STRATEGIES
Lack of social interest **Withdrawal**	• Carefully read the child's cues. Ask yourself questions such as these: » Are caregivers misreading signals or overwhelming the child? What does the child pay attention to? » Are there concerns about the child's vision or hearing? » How does the child respond to sensory stimulation? » Does the child have a history of neglect or abuse? » Does the child play with toys in the way in which they are intended to be played with? • Talk to your administrator about referring the child to her pediatrician. (See chapter 7 for more information about referrals.)
Clinginess **Excessive separation problems**	• Engage the child in an interesting activity right away; do not start the day with the most boring task. • Keep a family album or a single picture where the child can access it. • Allow for a transition or comfort item. • Maintain a predictable and posted schedule (picture schedules are great for young children) showing the sequence of the day. This helps children understand the passage of time and when their family member will return. • Be patient with the child. Avoid a "toughen them up" approach. The child is likely using you as a substitute family member for protection and nurturing, and verbal rejection such as, "Be a big girl," or "I'm everyone's teacher; you have to go play away from me" can backfire.

40

How Can I Help? A Teacher's Guide to Early Childhood Behavioral Health

BEHAVIOR	SAMPLE STRATEGIES
Sexual-behavior problems	• If the child is receiving therapy, respectfully ask her family members to obtain a current, signed release-of-information form and give a copy to you to keep on file. This signed form will enable you, the family, and the therapist to share observations and ideas for supporting the child. (See chapter 7 for more about release-of-information forms.) • Communicate with the child's family about therapy interventions that may need to be included in the classroom. • Reinforce appropriate physical boundaries and rules about safe and unsafe touch. You can use a program such as Stop, Go, and Tell for this purpose. • Remind children that our hands are for our own bodies, not for touching other people. • Behaviors such as touching one's own genitals in public, attempting to touch other children's or adults' genitals, or displaying age-inappropriate sexual knowledge can be symptoms of past trauma or ongoing problems with abuse or supervision. Gather more information to help you determine whether you need to report suspected maltreatment. • If a child masturbates in your classroom, have her wash her hands, and remind her to keep that behavior at home. • If a child draws something that concerns you, use open-ended questions, such as, "Tell me about this," to inquire about it. • Avoid interrogating or interviewing children on the spot. These conversations should take place in private.

CASE STUDY:
MARLI'S
FAMILY TRAUMA

Use what you have learned about trauma to work through the following scenario.

Marli is a three-year-old girl in your classroom. Over the last two weeks, she has been increasingly defiant, short-tempered, and quickly moved to tears. Once a good napper, she no longer sleeps at school and is frequently in a negative mood, saying no to almost anything anyone offers her. Additionally, you have noticed some regression in her behavior, including thumb sucking and baby talk. In the dramatic-play center, you observe her hitting a doll and saying, "Bad baby! Mommy's going to kill you and send you to heaven."

- What are your initial thoughts about Marli?

- What, if anything, do you do with Marli directly at this time?

Marli's mother (Nicolette) is expecting a baby soon, so Marli's grandmother (Cora) has been visiting the family over the last few weeks and has been picking up Marli from school. You have hesitated to speak to Cora because you do not know her well, and you have been waiting for Nicolette to resume picking Marli up so that you can talk about Marli's adjustment to the new baby. After observing Marli's play, however, you decide to speak to Cora.

During the conversation, you learn that Nicolette delivered her baby almost two weeks ago. Because of birth complications, both Nicolette and the baby had to be moved from the local hospital to one in a city nearly ninety minutes away. Cora explains that she has taken Marli there once to visit, but Marli was extremely upset and frightened when she saw Nicolette appearing so weak. Sadly, the baby passed away after ten days, and

42

How Can I Help? A Teacher's Guide to Early Childhood Behavioral Health

Nicolette is still in the hospital. Cora says that she and Marli's father have tried to keep the loss from Marli because she is too young to understand.

- What do you think Marli needs from her family right now?

- What do you think Marli needs from her teachers right now?

- What are some concrete ways that you can provide security and nurturing to Marli?

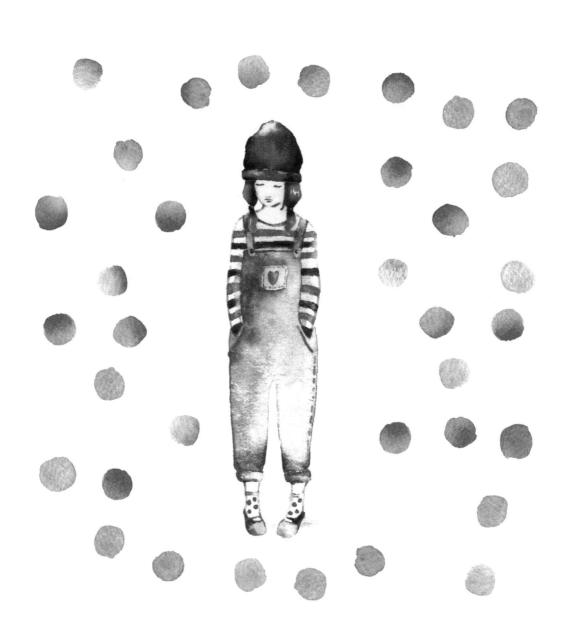

Mood Disorders
in Young Children

Mood disorders is an umbrella term that encompasses the many forms of depression, anxiety, and related disorders that affect people across the lifespan, including young children. Mood disorders are among the most common disorders diagnosed in the United States.

ANXIETY DISORDERS

Anxiety occurs throughout the lifespan and can serve developmentally appropriate functions. For instance, separation anxiety and stranger anxiety can keep a child safely near his attachment figure. However, for some children, typical anxiety can become problematic, or clinically significant anxiety can develop.

The DSM-5 includes multiple anxiety disorders beyond those covered here; however, here are three of the most common ones you may encounter in young children:

- Separation anxiety disorder
- Selective mutism
- Generalized anxiety disorder (GAD)

Let's further examine each of these disorders.

Separation Anxiety Disorder

According to Brenner Children's Hospital, separation anxiety (in which children tearfully protest being separated from their attachment figures) usually initially arises sometime between eight and twelve months. Though often frustrating, this phenomenon is typical, and the worst is usually over by the preschool years. In contrast, separation anxiety disorder can be diagnosed only when a child experiences separation anxiety outside of the developmentally appropriate period. Therefore, children at the upper ages of the early childhood period, around six through eight years old, are much more likely to receive this diagnosis than younger children. Additionally, symptoms of separation anxiety disorder must last for at least four weeks; this criterion is important to avoid pathologizing typical stress reactions associated with change.

What You May Notice

Separation anxiety disorder goes beyond children having trouble separating from their family members. This anxiety does not have to be rooted in an event or in fact; it can occur with or without a known trigger. Children with separation anxiety disorder may worry about their family members, resist going to child care or school (or other places), have trouble napping away from home, or experience physical pains as a result of their anxiety. They may have daily trouble getting to school or child care on time because they refuse to go, and once they arrive in their classrooms, they may take extra time to adjust to being there.

What You Can Do

Separation anxiety disorder can cause great distress for a child, his family members, and his teachers. Unfortunately, the reassurances that adults tend to offer at the moment of separation, such as saying, "It'll be okay," often do not really meet the child's needs. When working with a child who has separation anxiety disorder, consider using these strategies:

- Visit with the child's family members to discover how long this behavior has been occurring and whether family members have any suspicions about the root of the anxiety.

- Use predictable schedules, routines, and staffing patterns.

- Ensure that staffing patterns allow a nurturing and patient staff member to greet the child and his family member at arrival, facilitate the transition, and comfort the child after his family member leaves.

46

How Can I Help? A Teacher's Guide to Early Childhood Behavioral Health

- Determine whether the child is upset before arriving in the classroom or becomes upset at the actual point of separation. This is important for planning the timing of an intervention.

- Encourage the family member who drops off the child to engage with the child in a classroom activity for a moment, then have a staff member join the activity, and then have the family member leave.

When a Family Member Has Trouble Separating

Sometimes a child experiences separation anxiety because a family member shows anxiety about leaving the child. Remember that the family member, a critical part of the child's world, should also receive attention. Try these strategies:

- Acknowledge the family member's feelings: "It's hard to let someone else take care of your child."

- Normalize the family member's experience: "This is tough on family members. Many people feel anxious about leaving their children."

- Prepare the family member for the separation. Let him visit the center with the child before the child actually begins attending, and suggest concrete ideas for what will help with the separation and what will not.

- Provide information about how you and your colleagues help children who have difficulty separating from family members: "Many children cry for a few minutes. We work hard to engage them in play, and soon they calm down."

- Be proactive. A phone call, photo, or text to show that the child is doing well is worth its weight in gold. Be sure to get permission in advance to contact the family member in this way, and follow your program's policies for electronic communications about children.

Selective Mutism

Children with selective mutism may speak at home or in other places but not speak at all at child care or school. This lack of speaking does not stem from a speech or language problem and lasts beyond a brief period of adjusting to school. These children literally cannot speak at school or child care because of overwhelming anxiety.

What You May Notice

Many children speak in whispers, duck their heads, or hide behind family members when meeting a new adult for the first time. This type of shyness usually dissipates as the newness of attending school or child care wears off and a child becomes friendly with his teachers and other children.

However, for a child with selective mutism, even a whisper may be too much to expect. This behavior extends to an entire setting: the child does not speak to anyone, even a family member, in the school or child-care environment. Family members may report that the child speaks to them "all the time," but you do not observe him speaking at all. He may follow instructions or respond nonverbally but not utter a sound. As a result, you may have trouble assessing him because he does not read aloud or speak.

What You Can Do

- Check with the child's family members to find out whether he speaks in other places, has any history of communication issues, or has any diagnosed speech or language disorders.

- Make sure to communicate with the child in his primary language.

- Continue to speak with and communicate with the child both verbally and nonverbally. Do not force him to speak by either demanding directly or pressuring him through rewards or punishments.

- Avoid restricting the child's participation in your class or program. For instance, children with selective mutism should not be excluded from play or group times.

- Give the child time to adjust to your program. If he does not show increased efforts to communicate after approximately one month, refer him to a mental-health professional. Respectfully ask the child's family members to obtain a current, signed release-of-information form and give a copy to you to keep on file. This signed form will enable you, the family, and the professional to share observations and ideas for supporting the child. (See chapter 7 for more about referrals and release-of-information forms.)

- Reframe "will not speak" into "cannot speak." A child with selective mutism is not willfully choosing to not speak at school; subtle changes in our own language can keep us from blaming the child for the disorder.

- Share your guidance strategies with the child's family members. Emphasize that they should avoid punishment and bribery.

Generalized Anxiety Disorder (GAD)

Generalized anxiety disorder (GAD) cuts across the lifespan, although it more commonly affects adults than children. The DSM-5 notes that in GAD, feelings of worry persist over many situations for six months or longer, leaving individuals feeling restless, tired, and irritable and having problems with attention and concentration.

48

How Can I Help? A Teacher's Guide to Early Childhood Behavioral Health

What You May Notice

All children have fears; however, most fears cause limited disruption to children's lives and have a narrow focus (dogs, the dark, and so on). In contrast, generalized anxiety disorder is more pervasive and disruptive because it focuses more on children's worries about what *might* happen than on actual fears. Children may engage in anxious or regressive behaviors, such as crying, nail biting, hair twirling or chewing, or thumb sucking. Some children can verbally describe their fears and may confide in you. Others become upset when they see or hear things that represent their worries, even if they do not have the words to explain what is bothering them. Children with GAD may have irritable or angry interactions with others during stressful times.

What You Can Do

- Check with the child's family members about any changes they have noticed in him. Because anxiety in children can look like crankiness, fatigue, or inattentiveness, avoid asking only if the child "seems worried." Instead, focus on exploring all symptoms.

- As you visit with the child's family members, ask if anything has changed in his life or if any upsetting events have occurred.

- Maintain a predictable, consistent routine as much as possible.

- Teach the child calming strategies while acknowledging his distress: "I can hear that you're upset. Let's take a deep breath together right now."

- Look for patterns in the child's behavior to help you find possible sources of his anxiety. Does his irritability seem to go up right before nap time every day? Sleep is a vulnerable state, and a child with GAD may particularly feel the absence of his family members at nap time. Does a child get into conflicts with others near pick-up time? His worries may increase as other children's family members arrive but his own have not yet come.

● ●

For more information about anxiety in children,
visit **https://www.aacap.org/aacap/Families_and_Youth/
Facts_for_Families/FFF-Guide/The-Anxious-Child-047.aspx**

● ●

Teacher Task #1: Who's the Anxious One?

Anxiety disorders differ from *situational anxiety*, or temporary anxiety connected to specific circumstances, such as the nervousness that many people feel before giving a presentation. Situational anxiety is a relatively common experience among adults, yet it can cause us to have an incredibly difficult time communicating effectively. On the chart, fill in your thoughts, emotions, and physical reactions, such as increased heart rate, for each scenario. In the last column, write what you could do to manage your situational anxiety in each scenario so that you can communicate more effectively.

SCENARIO

A family member leaves a message on your work voicemail, saying that he is furious about his child getting head lice from your program and that he is meeting with your director today. The family member says that he and the director want to see you right after school.

WHAT YOU THINK	WHAT YOU FEEL	HOW YOUR BODY RESPONDS	HOW YOU CAN COPE

SCENARIO

A family member begs you to keep an important secret and then discloses that his child was abused over the weekend.

WHAT YOU THINK	WHAT YOU FEEL	HOW YOUR BODY RESPONDS	HOW YOU CAN COPE

How Can I Help? A Teacher's Guide to Early Childhood Behavioral Health

SCENARIO

**Your director asks you to confront a family member
whose weekly payment has been denied ... again.**

WHAT YOU THINK	WHAT YOU FEEL	HOW YOUR BODY RESPONDS	HOW YOU CAN COPE

SCENARIO

**A child in your class is out of diapers ... again. You plan to bring it up with the child's
mother at pick-up, but the child's father comes instead. He has previously insulted you,
calling you a "stupid babysitter," and you find him intimidating.**

WHAT YOU THINK	WHAT YOU FEEL	HOW YOUR BODY RESPONDS	HOW YOU CAN COPE

Now, reread what you wrote in the first three columns. If the scenarios in this exercise
caused you temporary discomfort or distress, imagine how it feels to be a child with GAD,
who constantly experiences similar but often more-intense reactions and emotions,
even in situations that others might consider benign, such as finding a ladybug in the
sand table.

DEPRESSIVE DISORDERS

Many people's ideas of depression derive from how adults with depression look and function. However, children who experience depression may look and function differently.

The DSM-5 includes a handful of depressive disorders. However, we will only examine the two that you will most likely encounter in young children:

- Disruptive mood regulation disorder (DMRD)
- Major depressive disorder (MDD)

Disruptive Mood Regulation Disorder (DMRD)

Disruptive mood regulation disorder (DMRD) is diagnosed in some children at the end of the early childhood period. The hallmark characteristics are ongoing irritable mood and disruptive behaviors in the long term.

What You May Notice

All young children have tantrums and can be disagreeable sometimes. However, a child with DMRD may be in an angry or irritable mood most of the time—not just temporarily or under certain circumstances. He may have tantrum-like behavior several times a week. He may also display symptoms similar to those of attention deficit hyperactivity disorder (ADHD) (see chapter 6) or some other disorder that involves mood swings and excessive anger. These symptoms are not transient; they characterize the child for at least one year. Children under age six do not qualify for this diagnosis.

What You Can Do

- Check with the child's family members to find out how long this behavior has been occurring, whether the child has any trauma history, and whether he has experienced recent changes or losses.

- While visiting with the family members, ask about the child's sleep patterns and whether he has had recent sleep disruptions. Poor sleep is a major contributor to overall poor functioning.

- Recognize that a young child cannot yet fully regulate his behavior. Every child has to learn this skill with help from adults (including you), and DMRD makes that learning especially challenging.

- When the child shows anger, narrate the emotional experience for him. For example, say, "You are so upset. It's hard to get yourself back together, and that's

52

How Can I Help? A Teacher's Guide to Early Childhood Behavioral Health

frustrating. Let's move over here so you can calm down." By doing these things, you model and teach the skills that will help the child ultimately learn to self-regulate, even if it is a very slow process.

- Refer the child to his pediatrician and to a mental-health professional. Respectfully ask the child's family members to obtain a current, signed release-of-information form for each provider and give copies to you to keep on file. These signed forms will enable you, the family, and the providers to share observations and ideas for supporting the child. (See chapter 7 for more about referrals and release-of-information forms.)

Major Depressive Disorder (MDD)

Major depressive disorder (MDD) is often simply called depression. According to Joan Luby, children as young as age three can suffer from depression, although an infant can also show symptoms of depression if his mother has this disorder. Medication is infrequently prescribed to treat MDD in very young children.

What You May Notice

All children are sometimes disagreeable, unhappy, or tearful, often in response to a loss or disappointment. However, a child with MDD may show many types of challenging behavior—such as aggressive, irritable, lethargic, disinterested, or sad and tearful—that do not relate to any particular event. He may seem emotionally unresponsive or have an apparent lack of facial and emotional expression. He might speak negatively toward others or himself ("I'm stupid" or "I hate you") and may even attempt to injure himself.

What You Can Do

- Communicate with the child's family members about any changes or upheavals in his family, including witnessing violence, separation from his primary caregivers, or existing depression or suicide attempts among family members.

- Teach the child emotion words to describe his behavior: "You're so frustrated right now. I'll help you feel safe."

- Avoid labeling the child by his behavior, such as by saying, "You're so mean," or "Don't act so ugly."

- Remember that depression can show itself through aggression and irritability as well as through lethargy and disinterest.

- Remind yourself that your role is to educate the child, not control him. A young child struggling with depression does not understand what is happening to him; he can benefit from education about moods, feelings, and social interactions to help him understand his experience.

- Children who suffer from depression often experience relationship problems. Work on building a nurturing and reliable relationship with the child to help buffer the effects of the disorder.

- Check your own behavior for ways in which the child may experience rejection at school. Do you find yourself avoiding a clingy child or sighing loudly when a child whines? A child with depression may interpret these signals as rejection, even if you do not direct them at him.

- Suicide in young children is rare, but it does happen. Alert the child's family members if he threatens to hurt himself or engages in self-injurious behaviors such as cutting, rubbing an eraser on himself until skin comes off, or biting himself.

- Refer the child to his pediatrician and to a mental-health professional who can provide formal screening. Respectfully ask the child's family members to obtain a current, signed release-of-information form for each provider and give copies to you to keep on file. These signed forms will enable you, the family, and the providers to share observations and ideas for supporting the child. (See chapter 7 for more about referrals and release-of-information forms.)

> For more information about depression in children, visit **https://www.aacap.org/aacap/Families_and_Youth/Resource_Centers/Depression_Resource_Center/Home.aspx**

- Check your classroom environment. Is this child being antagonized or picked on by others? Observe the child at play so you can intervene and model appropriate interactions while offering appropriate protections.

- Evaluate the child's social skills. For example, does he play with others with help but get into conflicts when an adult is not present? Model appropriate social skills and provide appropriate supervision.

Teacher Task #2: Talking to Children

How many of the sayings in the first column do you find yourself using? These phrases can harm children, whether or not they have depressive disorders. Practice replacing these sayings with sayings from the second column.

If you do not say any of the phrases in the first column, bravo! Instead, think about other things you frequently say to children. How might those words affect them, especially a child suffering from a depressive disorder? Use the second column as a guide to help you reframe or replace any troublesome phrases.

INSTEAD OF SAYING THIS ...	TRY SAYING THIS ...
"Are you crying again?"	"You're feeling so sad today."
"You're too big to be picked up."	"You need lots of hugs today."
"If you don't play with these toys, I'm throwing them all away!"	"You just want snuggles right now."
"Stop being so mean to your friends."	"You feel so frustrated."
"Calm yourself down."	"Let's take a deep breath together."
"I'm sending you to the director's office if you don't stop."	"Sometimes we just need a little break to feel better. Let's go to the calming area."
"If you throw one more toy, I'm telling your mom."	"Throwing isn't safe. I'm helping you to the soft area."

CASE STUDY:
LOLA'S ANXIETY SYMPTOMS

Use what you have learned about anxiety to work through the following scenario.

Six-year-old Lola has been in your class for three months. She has remained relatively quiet compared to the other children but has not shown any sort of behavior problem. Lola's mother, Reyna, has mentioned that last year, their family experienced a small house fire while Lola was present. Then, following a fire drill at school last week, Lola became so distressed, crying and breathing shallowly, that you could not calm her and called Reyna to come to school. Reyna reports that since that time, Lola has been crying before school, begging not to go.

Also since the fire drill, Lola has frequently arrived at school late and has complained almost daily of stomach pains and generally not feeling well. Every day this week, Lola has told you to call Reyna because Lola is supposed to go home early. You have talked to Reyna and know that she has not given any such instructions, and you are starting to feel frustrated with Lola's demands and complaints.

How do you proceed to help Lola and her family?

CHAPTER 5:

Disorders of Feeding, Toileting, and Sleeping in Young Children

Eating solid food, toilet training, and sleeping through the night represent important milestones in the early childhood period. They are also some of the most trying events of childhood for family members and caregivers, as these milestones typically arrive in challenging, "three-steps-forward-and-two-steps-back" ways. Sometimes, however, children experience difficulties in these areas that go beyond baby food spattered on the wall, soiled clothing, or loud cries at 2 a.m. When issues with feeding, toileting, and sleeping interfere with a child's growth, well-being, and quality of life, typical development may veer off course and result in a disorder.

DISORDERS OF FEEDING

Disorders of feeding range from the ingestion of inappropriate objects to regurgitation to serious food refusal. While other disorders of feeding, such as anorexia and bulimia, exist, they do not commonly affect young children. This part of the chapter examines three common disorders of feeding in the early childhood period:

- Pica

- Rumination disorder

- Avoidant restrictive food intake disorder (ARFID)

Pica

Pica is a type of disordered eating in which a child persistently eats nonfood substances. *Nonfood substances* include anything that is not food: rocks, bottle caps, hair, and so on. This disorder sometimes occurs along with others, such as intellectual disability or autism spectrum disorder (see chapter 6). David McAdam and his colleagues point out that pica poses serious dangers because the nonfood items a child ingests may damage her gastrointestinal system and expose her to hazardous materials and bacteria.

What You May Notice

Children under two years old typically explore the world by putting objects in their mouths. But a child with pica continues to mouth and even ingest nonfood items beyond age two. This means that a child in your care who has pica might consume classroom materials, such as checkers, crayons, paper towels, or any other item that she can swallow.

What You Can Do

- Always keep your classroom free of choking hazards.

- Communicate with the child's family members about any eating problems she may have and any history of this behavior in other settings.

- Refer the child to her pediatrician and to a mental-health professional. Respectfully ask the child's family members to obtain a current, signed release-of-information form for each provider and give copies to you to keep on file. These signed forms will enable you, the family, and the providers to share observations and ideas for supporting the child. (See chapter 7 for more about referrals and release-of-information forms.)

- Closely monitor the child's activities and play materials.

Rumination Disorder

Infants and young children with rumination disorder may ingest food and then bring it back up into the mouth to spit it out, rechew it, reswallow it, or all three. This rare disorder can result in problems with growth and nutrition because these children's bodies are unable to use the nutrients in the food. Other complications include dental problems, choking, and stomach problems.

58

How Can I Help? A Teacher's Guide to Early Childhood Behavioral Health

What You May Notice

Young children generally exert control over their eating behaviors. They may be picky, have sensory sensitivities, and eat better in one setting than in another. However, rumination disorder goes beyond these typical eating difficulties. You will usually notice choking, gagging, or vomiting in children with this disorder, and in the long term, you may see them experiencing delayed growth, low weight, or evidence of possible intellectual disability.

What You Can Do

- Communicate with the child's family members and other caregivers about other occurrences of this behavior.

- Monitor the child closely for problems with choking.

- Refer the child to her pediatrician. Respectfully ask the child's family members to obtain a current, signed release-of-information form and give a copy to you to keep on file. This signed form will enable you, the family, and the pediatrician to share observations and ideas for supporting the child. (See chapter 7 for more about referrals and release-of-information forms.)

Avoidant Restrictive Food Intake Disorder (ARFID)

Picky eating is a hallmark of early childhood, and typical eating patterns include eating jags, such as wanting to eat only fish sticks for a month, then wanting to eat only chicken nuggets; sensitivities to textures, flavors, and temperatures; and frequently changing favorite foods. However, avoidant restrictive food intake disorder (ARFID) is more extreme than these typical, albeit sometimes trying, behaviors. Children with ARFID avoid eating to the point that they may experience growth problems and may get their only nutrition from consuming liquid nutritional supplements. They have access to suitable food, but they continue to avoid eating.

What You May Notice

Though all children exhibit disrupted eating at some point, most children will eat some foods during the day. In fact, pleasant meal times at school often result in children trying more new and different foods than they will for their families. However, children with ARFID will simply not consume food. They may be underweight or have symptoms of poor nutrition, such as thinning hair, and may already be under a doctor's care. They may have medical permission to access their liquid nutritional supplements during school times.

What You Can Do

- When having a pre-enrollment meeting with a child's family members, ask them about the child's preferred and avoided foods, any food allergies or sensitivities she has, any nutritional supplements she takes, and the family's feeding practices, such as whether they eat at a table. Most children acquire the label "picky eater" at some point in their lives, but the knowledge you gain from these conversations may help you identify children who refuse food or exist only on nutritional supplements.

- During this meeting, if you learn that the child has atypical eating or signs of ARFID, suggest that her family members consult her pediatrician for guidance before enrolling the child in your program. Respectfully ask the family members to obtain a current, signed release-of-information form and give a copy to you to keep on file. This signed form will enable you, the family, and the pediatrician to share observations and ideas for supporting the child. (See chapter 7 for more about referrals and release-of-information forms.)

- Even if the child refuses food in your classroom, encourage her to participate in typical eating practices, such as sitting at a table with the other children.

- Avoid force-feeding or trying to feed infants in their sleep.

- Avoid bribes or punishments related to food and eating.

- Remember that progress comes in small steps. A child who will touch food and then touch her face is one step closer to eating.

- Model best eating practices. Whenever possible, one teacher should sit with the children at snack time and mealtime and model appropriate eating and interactions.

• •

For more information about the disorders
of feeding discussed in this book, visit
**https://www.nationaleatingdisorders.org/
information-eating-disorder**

• •

DISORDERS OF TOILETING

According to Johns Hopkins Medicine, a child normally achieves control of her bladder and bowels between twenty-four and thirty months. However, there is substantial variation, and incidents such as bedwetting can continue to happen sporadically throughout childhood. For some children, this lack of control is voluntary, while others have no ability to control their elimination schedules or locations. When this failure is

60

How Can I Help? A Teacher's Guide to Early Childhood Behavioral Health

related to bladder control and occurs at age five or older, it is known as *enuresis*, which may be classified as nocturnal (occurring during the night), diurnal (occurring during the day), or both. When the failure is related to bowel control and occurs at age four or older, it is called *encopresis*. (Note that according to the DSM-5, toileting problems associated with a medical condition do not qualify as either of these disorders.) Both types of disorders can have physiological causes, such as sleep problems or bladder abnormalities, but emotional and relationship factors can also contribute.

What You May Notice

The window for appropriate toilet training varies by the readiness and interest of the child but generally ranges from eighteen to thirty-six months, with the majority of children out of diapers by forty-two months. A child with a disorder of toileting may have poor appetite and complain of stomach pain. She may go to the bathroom less frequently or have fewer bowel movements than expected. She may continue to void in her diapers or clothing, either while awake or during naps. She may even go to locations other than the bathroom to empty her bowels or bladder and may or may not hide what she has done. Children who suffer from encopresis can become impacted, resulting in both constipation and bowel leakage, which can look like diarrhea. However, constipation can also make it difficult or painful for children to move their bowels and can contribute to enuresis.

For a developmentally appropriate review of toileting practices, visit **https://www.zerotothree.org/resources/266-potty-training-learning-to-the-use-the-toilet**

What You Can Do

- Communicate with the child's family members about developmentally appropriate methods for toilet training, and educate them about signs of readiness.

- Assess the emotional context in which the disorder occurs. Relationship challenges and tension can contribute to toileting problems.

- Refer the child to her pediatrician and to a child-development specialist. Respectfully ask the child's family members to obtain a current, signed release-of-information form for each provider and give copies to you to keep on file. These signed forms will enable you, the family, and the providers to share observations and ideas for supporting the child. (See chapter 7 for more about referrals and release-of-information forms.)

- Monitor your emotional relationship with the child. Make sure it is positive and that toileting issues do not become the focus of the relationship.

- Avoid punishments and bribing for toileting behaviors.

DISORDERS OF SLEEPING

Early childhood teachers may be affected by a child's sleep problems directly, such as when she has difficulty transitioning into or taking a nap, or indirectly, such as when she has poor overnight sleep and then is irritable and hits other children. All children occasionally have episodes of poor sleep because of changes in routine, growth, or illness, but when a child persistently fails to get the sleep she needs, a disorder of sleeping may be the root cause.

Sleep Guidelines

In the article "Healthy Sleep Habits," the American Academy of Pediatrics provides these guidelines for how much a child of a given age should sleep:

AGE	DAILY AMOUNT OF SLEEP NEEDED
4–12 months	12–16 hours
1–2 years	11–14 hours
3–5 years	10–13 hours
6–12 years	9–12 hours

A good night's sleep is critical to a child's (and an adult's) overall health. To get that kind of sleep, a child requires good sleep hygiene: a bedtime routine that sets the stage for good sleep, a safe and appropriate place to sleep, and the ability to get enough sleep at night. This means that adults need to help children go to bed on time, limit screen time before bed, and take time to be quiet and calm before falling asleep.

How Can I Help? A Teacher's Guide to Early Childhood Behavioral Health

For more information on children's sleep, visit
**https://www.sleepfoundation.org/
articles/children-and-sleep**

When babies sleep, they typically wake every few hours, most noticeably at night, to eat or have other needs met. Though they need greater amounts of sleep than older children or adults, they take that sleep in much smaller segments. In fact, sleeping "through the night," an achievement that many babies still have not met by six months, means that the baby can sleep for five hours straight. Such uneven sleep patterns are typical (though often exhausting for adults). Insufficient amounts of sleep, on the other hand, can mean that a child persistently struggles to fall asleep, wakes up too early and cannot go back to sleep, or has trouble staying asleep through the night.

Teacher Task #1: Sleep Calculations

Help family members calculate the entire amount of time that their child needs for bedtime preparation and actual sleep. For example, four-year-old Rangi needs to get up at 7:00 a.m. to get ready for child care and needs ten to twelve hours of sleep. It takes him thirty minutes to fall asleep once he is in bed, and the preparations—his bath, tooth brushing, and bedtime story—take one hour. Therefore, Rangi needs to start his bedtime routine at 7:30 p.m. to get ten hours of sleep or at 5:30 p.m. to get twelve hours of sleep. This is a surprising calculation for most families!

What You May Notice

Children who fail to get sufficient sleep may look tired or fatigued. They may be irritable, moody, or emotionally unstable. They might yawn and show signs of daytime sleepiness even after they have given up daytime naps. These children may have poor attention and concentration and show regressive behaviors, such as thumb-sucking. They may have trouble arriving at school on time. They may even struggle at nap time because they are so tired that they actually have difficulty falling asleep.

What You Can Do

Toddlers and older children often resist sleep; after all, once they figure out that adults stay up later, they want to be in on the fun! Toddlers and older children need assistance in preparing for bed, adhering to bedtime routines and schedules, and maintaining safe places to sleep. Adults must create appropriate sleep environments for children, even though a given child might not want to sleep and might protest, "I'm not tired!"

- Provide the family members of all children with recommended sleep amounts based on each child's age.

- Educate family members about best practices in sleep hygiene for children and the importance of sleep for growth and health.

- Ensure that families have opportunities to learn about the importance of sleep routines, limited pre-bedtime screen time, and safe sleep. Safe-sleep topics should include how to create a safe sleeping space for infants (that is, no bumpers, blankets, or toys in the child's crib and no bed sharing when she is young)* and how to reduce the risk of sudden unexpected infant death (SUID), including laying infants on their backs to sleep unless a physician has directed otherwise.

   ***Note:** Bed sharing is a safety issue for young infants because, if their faces become covered by the bedclothes or if someone accidentally rolls over on them, they are not strong enough to clear their own airways and can suffocate. However, many families of toddlers and preschoolers choose to bed share and do it safely and successfully.

- Maintain a safe-sleep environment in your classroom, ensuring that sleeping children are supervised by sight and sound at all times.

- Provide a place for children to rest as needed, even if it is just a quiet spot in the classroom.

- If a child shows unusual sleepiness, observe her for other signs of poor health.

- Refer the child to her pediatrician and to a child-development specialist if symptoms continue. Also refer her to a sensory-informed occupational therapist if she shows signs of sensory-integration problems, such as sensitivity to certain types of light, sound, movement, or touch. Respectfully ask the child's family members to obtain a current, signed release-of-information form for each provider and give copies to you to keep on file. These signed forms will enable you, the family, and the providers to share observations and ideas for supporting the child. (See chapter 7 for more about referrals and release-of-information forms.)

- If a child is extremely fatigued, has poor muscle tone or control, or becomes minimally responsive or completely unresponsive, get emergency medical care for her.

64

How Can I Help? A Teacher's Guide to Early Childhood Behavioral Health

Parasomnias

Many families have encountered the troubling disorders of sleeping called parasomnias. Symptoms tend to occur during the night, so you might not personally experience these disorders with the children in your care, but you might hear about them from family members. This category includes these conditions:

- Sleepwalking
- Sleep terrors (sometimes called night terrors)
- Nightmare disorder

Sleepwalking involves a child getting out of bed and walking around while still asleep; sleep terrors involve a deeply asleep child seeming to be in a state of panic. In either case, according to the articles "Night Terrors, Sleep Terrors" and "Sleep Walking" by the American Sleep Association, the child does not need to be awakened. She may not remember the event or any specific dreams, and waking her will only distress her. Sleepwalking often causes supervision concerns to family members, while sleep terrors are frightening for them but not necessarily for the child, who may not be aware of her apparently panicked state. Both of these disorders have strong genetic components.

Nightmare disorder is the recurrent experience of having alarming dreams. The DSM-5 states that up to 3.9 percent of preschoolers may suffer from regular nightmares. Unlike a child who sleepwalks or has sleep terrors, a child with nightmare disorder does wake up during episodes of the disorder, often with keen recollections of the frightening images from her dreams. This pattern, obviously, causes sleep disruption and also relates to problems such as fears of going to bed, a lack of sufficient sleep, and daytime sleepiness.

What You May Notice

Teachers may not ever directly experience parasomnias in a child. However, they might notice daytime sleepiness in a child who is having nightmares, or (more likely) they might serve as sources of information for family members whose children are experiencing parasomnias.

What You Can Do

- For sleepwalking and sleep terrors, provide family members with information about helping a child get back into bed, settle down, or both without waking (and thereby distressing) the child. Sleep terrors generally subside by the preschool years, but sleepwalking can last a lifetime, though the duration varies greatly from person to person.

- When a child experiences sleep terrors, her distressed cries may awaken and frighten her siblings. Educate family members about how to soothe and manage these other children.

- For sleepwalking concerns, work with the child's family members to arrange safe home and classroom environments and to observe whether the child has other unusual behaviors, such as sleep eating.

- For nightmare disorder, check with the child's family members about any trauma history. Traumatizing events can cause recurrent nightmares.

- Should a child have a nightmare while in your care, patiently reassure her and help reorient her to reality: she is at school or child care with you, and she is safe.

- Children are often interested in their dreams and may enjoy drawing some pleasant ones. If a child draws her nightmares, ask her to also draw a solution to each nightmare. For example, a child who draws a nightmare of a villain chasing her can then draw herself in a cape, flying away like a superhero. These types of images are most powerful when the child creates them.

- Provide family members with education about appropriate media use. Frightening images from television, tablets, and movies are very real to children and can make their way into dreams.

· ·

For more information about infant sleep, consult this excellent resource from Stanford Children's Health:
https://www.stanfordchildrens.org/ en/topic/default?id=infant-sleep-90-P02237

· ·

CASE STUDY:
ELI'S DISRUPTED SLEEP

Use what you have learned about children and sleep to work through the following scenario.

Twenty-two-month-old Eli will join your program in the fall. During the standard pre-enrollment meeting with his parents, you ask about Eli's sleep routine. The parents tell you that Eli usually goes to bed around 11:00 p.m. and usually gets up around 9:00 a.m. He does not nap unless he happens to fall asleep on his own in the afternoon. Eli likes to watch TV in bed, and his parents have put a television in his bedroom so that he can watch until he falls asleep. They indicate that they only allow him to watch children's TV shows, however.

When you ask further questions, the parents tell you that this sleep pattern developed because Eli's father, Ron, works two jobs, one of which is a graveyard shift. Because Eli's mother also works full time, Eli stays with his grandmother during the day so Ron can sleep when he gets home. Thus, the only time Ron can spend with Eli is late at night. The parents laugh and tell you that someone is always awake at their house, and someone is always asleep.

- What are your thoughts on Eli's sleep patterns, sleep needs, and sleep hygiene?

- How would you approach this family about meeting Eli's sleep needs?

- What do you think Eli's parents need to know about the sleep routine that he will find at school?

CHAPTER 6:

Neurodevelopmental Disorders in Young Children

The first chapter in the DSM-5 contains a collection of related disorders that all begin early in life and cause developmental challenges for the children they affect. This category of mental-health concerns is called neurodevelopmental disorders. Neurodevelopmental disorders are brain-based difficulties that affect a wide variety of social and intellectual skills.

Teacher Task #1: Exploring Executive Functioning

Many children with neurodevelopmental disorders struggle with executive functioning, which includes skills such as paying attention, getting organized, and remembering details. To help you empathize with these children and to enhance your awareness of how these skills affect behavior, this exercise will help you learn about your own executive functioning.

Visit **http://www.LDonline.org/article/29122** and rate yourself on a scale from 1 (lowest) to 10 (highest) for each of these executive-functioning characteristics:

- Inhibition
- Shift
- Emotional control
- Initiation
- Working memory

- Planning/organization

- Organization of materials

- Self-monitoring

NEURODEVELOPMENTAL DISORDERS

Here are some of the most common neurodevelopmental disorders you might encounter as an early childhood teacher:

- Intellectual disability (ID) or intellectual developmental disorder (IDD)

- Global developmental delay (GDD)

- Autism spectrum disorder (ASD)

- Attention deficit hyperactivity disorder (ADHD)

Let's look at each of these disorders more closely.

Intellectual Disability (ID) or Intellectual Developmental Disorder (IDD)

In the report *Highlights of Changes from DSM-IV-TR to DSM-5*, the American Psychiatric Association states that the term intellectual disability (ID)—also called intellectual developmental disorder (IDD)—has taken the place of the older term *mental retardation*. From early in life, an individual with ID has deficits both in academic learning and in adaptive skills (also known as self-help skills, adaptive functioning, or self-care skills). These problems exist in more than one setting—for example, at home and at school. A diagnosis of ID also contains a specifier that indicates the severity of the person's deficits in adaptive skills: mild, moderate, severe, or profound. Because a mental-health professional must complete certain assessment measures to diagnose ID, a child who comes to your class with this diagnosis will have a formal record of testing and observations.

What You May Notice

A child with ID may need more time to accomplish a task than his peers of the same age do, or he may seem younger than his chronological age and exhibit developmental delays. He may engage in more sensory-focused behaviors than his peers do or may have challenges establishing friendships.

70

How Can I Help? A Teacher's Guide to Early Childhood Behavioral Health

What You Can Do

Like all children, a child with ID is unique, and his learning and assessment should be personalized. Remember, the specifier in his diagnosis represents the difficulties that he has with adaptive, not cognitive, skills. As a teacher, you will need to create scaffolds for the child to help him build his self-help skills and grow toward independence.

Remember the whole child, not just the diagnosis, and be aware of the natural ways in which skills overlap during activities, giving you opportunities to better assess the child's abilities. For instance, imagine that your class is engaging in a fruit-tasting activity as part of a unit on nutrition. The objective for most of the children is to describe different tastes and textures. A child with ID might not have the oral-language skills to meet this objective; which of his other skills could you measure through this activity? Consider these possibilities:

Social-emotional skills
- Waiting to be served
- Sharing
- Participating actively or passively in conversation

Sensory experiences
- Examining colors
- Smelling various scents
- Exploring textures

Though they are not skills per se, sensory experiences are important ways to reach and teach children with ID, as they take much longer to develop abstract thinking skills than their typically developing peers do.

Motor skills
- Passing fruit to a friend
- Preparing fruit, such as peeling an orange or pulling grapes off their stems

Self-help skills
- Feeding oneself
- Gathering needed supplies
- Taking trash to the trash can

Perhaps this child does not spontaneously describe fruit as "sour" or "squishy," as some of the other children do, but we can miss subtle bits of progress if we focus only on the primary goal. For each child and each activity, we should measure skills and abilities that are appropriate for the child's developmental age, even if they differ from what is appropriate for his chronological age.

As a more specific example, imagine that you are conducting the fruit-tasting activity with a child who has ID and is chronologically four years old but has a developmental age of six months. Rather than assessing this child on his ability to name or describe a fruit (developmentally appropriate skills for a four-year-old), you could assess him on his ability to reach for the fruit, get it to his mouth, or show pleasure at the texture (developmentally appropriate skills for a six-month-old).

Global Developmental Delay (GDD)

If a child under the age of five is functioning overall at a developmental level below the typical range for his chronological age, he may receive a temporary diagnosis of global developmental delay (GDD). This diagnosis can be applied when a child cannot yet complete the formal assessment procedures required for other diagnoses (for example, if he does not yet have the verbal, motor, or cognitive skills to respond to or engage with assessment materials). However, a child with GDD will eventually need to be reassessed to determine a more specific diagnosis, as GDD cannot be diagnosed in children over age five.

What You May Notice

A child with GDD may function at a level delayed from his chronological age. He may learn at a different rate from his peers and process information more slowly than they do.

What You Can Do

- Make sure to help the child grow in all developmental domains and to measure his progress from where he is rather than from where he ought to be.

- Remember that a solid teacher-child relationship is the foundation for all other cognitive skills.

- Attend to the child's sensory needs. For example, he may benefit from additional movement opportunities during the day.

72

How Can I Help? A Teacher's Guide to Early Childhood Behavioral Health

- For a child under three years, encourage his family to help him participate in an early intervention program.

- Encourage the family to communicate with the child's pediatrician about developmental progress or concerns.

Autism Spectrum Disorder (ASD)

Autism spectrum disorder (ASD) is the current diagnostic term used in the DSM-5, replacing older terms such as *Asperger's*, *pervasive developmental disorder*, or *high-functioning autism*. This new term emphasizes that autism is more accurately conceptualized as a spectrum instead of a series of discrete but related diagnoses. Children with ASD have widely varied intellectual abilities, with some children experiencing intellectual disabilities and others being identified as academically gifted.

> According to the National Education Association, children who have an identified disability and are identified as academically gifted are often called *twice exceptional*.

When a child is diagnosed with ASD, the diagnosis contains several other pieces of information:

- Whether or not the child has an intellectual impairment

- Whether or not the child has a language impairment

- A level specifier (1, 2, or 3). As the DSM-5 explains, this specifier indicates how much support the child needs for overall functioning, with level 3 requiring the most support.

What You May Notice

Children with ASD often struggle to manage and process sensory input. For instance, a typically developing child might simply notice the siren of a passing fire truck, whereas a child with ASD might become very agitated because to him, that same siren is painfully loud. A typically developing child also reads subtle social cues, such as facial expressions, in much the same way as an adult would. A child with ASD, on the other hand, might have difficulty accurately interpreting these cues.

Regardless of the specifics of their diagnoses, many children with ASD share common challenges. They typically struggle with social-emotional communication and relationship building. They may engage in repetitive acts or speech, such as spinning wheels on toys, rocking back and forth, or repeating others' words (note that this last behavior is also common in typically developing infants). They often have rigid, inflexible behavior, restricted interests or activities, and unusual sensory interests or sensitivities.

What You Can Do

- Attend to the child's individual challenges in communication by giving him direct instruction on social skills. For instance, he may need your help learning to read facial expressions and other social cues.

- Help the child manage his sensory needs. Reduce visual or auditory clutter in the classroom, and consult a sensory-informed occupational therapist to learn about evidenced-based interventions that you can provide for sensory needs.

- Be aware that the child may intensely dislike change. Assist and comfort him through any disruptions in classroom routines, including having comfort items available. When possible, inform him in advance about upcoming changes (even temporary ones) and help him prepare for them.

Attention Deficit Hyperactivity Disorder (ADHD)

According to the DSM-5, attention deficit hyperactivity disorder (ADHD) has replaced the older term *attention deficit disorder* (ADD). ADHD can cause children to have difficulties with hyperactivity and impulsivity, inattentiveness, or all of these areas. When a child is diagnosed with ADHD, the mental-health professional includes a specifier that indicates which type or types of symptoms predominate in that child. Approximately 5 percent of American children are diagnosed with ADHD.

What You May Notice

Young children often struggle because adults have developmentally inappropriate expectations for them, and even a typically developing child can demonstrate impulsive and agitated behaviors when he encounters rigid settings. All young children require lots of opportunities for movement and hands-on play, breaks every few minutes, and generous praise and reinforcement for demonstrating desirable behaviors, such as sharing and waiting their turn. A child with ADHD may display developmentally inappropriate behaviors for his age, including fidgeting, daydreaming, or struggling to sit still, wait his turn, stay in his seat, or regulate his behavior. He might blurt out answers, fail to pay careful attention, or miss out on instructions. Remember, all young children display these behaviors sometimes, but in a child with ADHD, these behaviors occur consistently in multiple settings and are not appropriate for the child's developmental age.

What You Can Do

- Researchers Alice Charach and her colleagues note that some of the most effective interventions for helping young children manage ADHD symptoms are programs that provide support and training to family members. Even if your organization does not have a formal program for this purpose, you can provide family members with information on developmentally appropriate behaviors and expectations, and you can model developmentally appropriate guidance strategies.

- Model for the child how to sustain attention, inhibit impulses, delay gratification, and be still for long periods of time.

- Help the child practice these skills, and reinforce him when he demonstrates them.

- Remember that symptoms of trauma exposure can mimic disorders such as ADHD, and symptoms of early severe neglect can look a lot like ASD. Start by checking with the child's family members to see if he has a trauma history.

- If the child does not yet have a formal diagnosis, refer him to a mental-health professional. Respectfully ask the child's family members to obtain a current, signed release-of-information form and give a copy to you to keep on file. This signed form will enable you, the family, and the professional to share observations and ideas for supporting the child. (See chapter 7 for more about referrals and release-of-information forms.)

- If the child's family members choose to have him evaluated by medical or mental-health professionals, be prepared to help the process move along by completing questionnaires or speaking with professionals. (See chapter 7 for more about this process.)

- Observe the child to gain more information about his symptoms and skills. How long will he sit and engage in group time? building with blocks? art activities? lunch or snack? How does he respond to a verbal instruction when he is looking at you? when he is not looking at you?

- Accept small, nondisruptive needs for movement, such as leg shaking or fidgeting. Children, particularly ones with neurodevelopmental disorders, must move.

- Break activities into smaller, more-frequent chunks with opportunities for movement in between.

- Never withdraw physical activity as a punishment.

- Praise the child often. Use specific praise whenever possible, such as, "Thank you for coming to the carpet right away," or "I love that you're spending so much time on your drawing."

- Provide a predictable routine.

- Provide a visual schedule that uses pictures to illustrate the order of activities. Even typically developing children can have problems with remembering the daily routine. Having a visual reminder will help everyone.

- Provide timers to help children manage waiting. Time appears much longer to children than it does to adults.

- Limit transitions. How much time in your classroom day is spent simply getting from one activity to another? This includes processes such as lining up, washing hands, going outside, or packing up to go home. Eliminate any unnecessary transitions. Fill the remaining ones with singing or quick games so that children are not simply left waiting, and work to integrate those transitions smoothly into your day.

- Build a relationship with the child. Spending a few minutes each day just in pleasant interaction with him can make a huge difference.

- Keep track of the child's progress. Change can happen so subtly or gradually that we do not notice it occurring. Recording goals and even the smallest steps that the child takes toward them—such when he reduces his number of peer conflicts from twelve per day to ten per day—can actually mean a lot!

- Remember that every child (and adult) has bad days, such as when he has had too little sleep or feels ill. Are you keeping track of typical days and "other" days?

- Evaluate your classroom environment for improvements you could make. Is your room calm? Is the furniture arranged to discourage running? How loud is your voice? How upbeat or calming is the music you play? When you work in your classroom with the children, do you feel calm or frenzied (remember, your mood affects the children's moods)?

CASE STUDY:
JOHNNY IN PERPETUAL MOTION

Three-year-old Johnny has been in your class for four months but has never attended other child care. You have become frustrated with the amount of energy you spend to keep him focused in the classroom. Johnny frequently gets out of his chair, often going to the block table to build without permission. He often seems to not even hear you until you go to him and physically touch his shoulder. He is active on the playground but has not yet made any friends with whom he engages in interactive or pretend

76

How Can I Help? A Teacher's Guide to Early Childhood Behavioral Health

play. Johnny also has a habit of chewing on things, especially pencils and crayons, and sometimes when you ask him to draw, he will simply sit and chew instead. Even when he is sitting (which is not often!), he is constantly in motion, chewing or tapping objects or fidgeting.

- What are your hypotheses about Johnny's behavior?

- What else do you need to know?

- Though you do not currently know whether Johnny has a diagnosed disorder, what steps could you take to help Johnny in the classroom?

- How would you proceed from here?

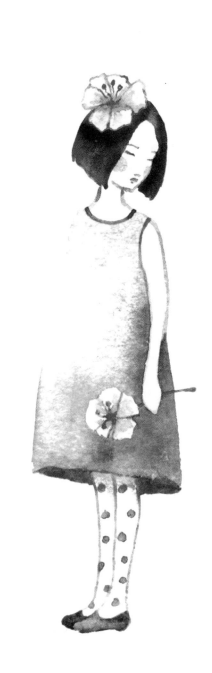

CHAPTER 7:

The Referral and Assessment Process

The processes of psychological referral and assessment can seem vague and distant to many teachers, who often work on the periphery of these events. However, when a child is referred for services or an assessment, the teacher is an integral part of the process and may be involved in making a referral, providing information for an assessment, and applying recommended strategies in the classroom. Quality early childhood assessment involves a systematic examination of the child's functioning across developmental domains and settings.

DO I NEED TO REFER THIS CHILD?

You might consider making a referral to another professional when a child exhibits concerning behaviors, such as those listed in previous chapters, and the symptoms do not improve despite your efforts to use best practices. For example, you would not need to refer an eleven-month-old who will not stay with the group at circle time or who does not eat neatly with a spoon; these expectations are developmentally inappropriate for an eleven-month-old. However, a two-year-old who does not speak or play with toys, even after months in your care, could benefit from the analysis of an additional professional.

HOW THE REFERRAL AND ASSESSMENT PROCESS WORKS

In most child-care facilities, referrals are normally made to private providers not affiliated with your program. If you work in a school system, your school may have policies, procedures, and even providers already set up for the referral process. If so, follow these guidelines carefully.

Either way, be absolutely clear about what you say in your official role as an employee, and always consult with your administration as you begin to consider the need for a referral. If you suggest to family members in your official capacity that a child needs additional services (for example, if you say, "Your child has [diagnosis]. You need to take her to a doctor"), you could make your program liable to pay for those services. Use language that clearly shows that you are not requiring family members to take a particular action. For example, you might say, "I'm seeing [behavior that concerns you]. I suggest that you see [an applicable professional] to get more information."

The following summary describes what may occur when you decide to refer a child for further evaluation.

Step 1: Talking to Family Members

Before you decide to make a referral, talk to your administrator, and communicate with the child's family about your concerns (see chapter 8 for tips on communicating with family members). Remember, these are difficult conversations to have with families, and many family members fear being judged as "bad" caregivers or having their child "labeled" or put on medication. Emphasize that, just as the family members do, you want what is best for the child, so you would like to learn more about her and how to help her more effectively in your classroom. Find out whether the family members are also concerned about the child's behavior and, if so, what their specific concerns are. Explain that there are professionals who could help provide more information about the behavior.

Step 2: Making a Referral

Once you decide to go ahead with the referral, you need to decide to whom you will refer the child. A good start is to make a referral to the child's pediatrician, who can then

80

How Can I Help? A Teacher's Guide to Early Childhood Behavioral Health

direct the family to specialized providers, such as therapists, if needed. Your program might also keep lists of specialized providers available, but avoid the appearance of endorsing certain professionals or benefitting from referrals; for example, if your spouse is a psychologist, referring children to him or her for evaluation would be a conflict of interest. Respectfully ask the child's family members to obtain a current, signed release-of-information form for each provider and give copies to you to keep on file. These signed forms will enable you to share your observations and concerns with these professionals and fully participate in the assessment process.

Once you know to whom you will refer the child, make sure your information is clear, concise, and organized so that you can quickly provide it when requested. The staff at a provider's office will not have large blocks of time to talk with you or look through volumes of notes. To organize your thoughts, start by considering a few different ways to describe your concerns about the child's behavior. These concerns could fall into several different categories.

Positive Difficulties and Negative Abilities

First, try categorizing your observations as positive or negative—that is, are you concerned about what the child *is* doing (positive difficulties) or about what the child *is not* doing (negative abilities)? The following table provides some examples of each type of concern. In some cases, a child both exhibits troubling behaviors *and* has not met typical developmental milestones for her age.

POSITIVE (PRESENT) DIFFICULTIES	NEGATIVE (ABSENT) ABILITIES
• "Tariq hits and bites other children." • "Josie destroys books."	• "Riley does not make eye contact." • "Zora does not yet feed herself."

The Child's Relationships

A second way to categorize your concerns is to describe how the child relates to others. Include concrete observations about how she functions when alone and how she interacts with family members, teachers, other children, and strangers. For example, have you noticed that a child has conflict only with other children? Does she lack a developmentally appropriate fear of strangers? Does a three-year-old prefer to play only by herself, seeming not to notice others?

Sometimes your concerns about relationships may not focus solely on the child. For instance, a two-year-old may seem to have developmentally appropriate social skills, but you suspect that her caregivers misinterpret her cues or relate and respond to her inappropriately. Thus, the family, not just the child, may be your primary source of concern in this situation.

Prevention and Adjustment

Some of the most challenging concerns to put into words are those about preventing problems or adjusting to new circumstances. Perhaps, for instance, a child in your care recently acquired two older step-siblings and is no longer an only child. Maybe another child was recently placed in a foster home. Yet another child may have witnessed domestic violence and moved with her mother to a new home. These children may show difficulties with sleeping, toileting, or behavior that you might attribute to natural but short-term adjustment problems. But even if these children do not display behavioral problems, you may be concerned about how they will adapt to their new circumstances.

Is there a place in the referral system for children like these? Absolutely. You can refer a child in such circumstances to a psychologist or, in the case of primary prevention, to a child-development or child-guidance specialist who does not rely on insurance reimbursement. Remember that insurance usually requires a diagnosis to reimburse a provider, so in cases in which the child may not have a diagnosable disorder, a child-development specialist is the best bet.

Teacher Task #1: Describing a Child for a Referral

Think about a child whom you care for and about whom you have concerns. Avoiding any formal diagnostic language, describe that child by answering these questions:

- What is this child *doing* that concerns you?
- What is this child *not doing* that concerns you?
- Does this child have unusual amounts of conflict with teachers, family members, or peers?
- Does this child seem uninterested in expected relationships? (For instance, does she play only by herself at an age when she would typically play with other children?)

82

How Can I Help? A Teacher's Guide to Early Childhood Behavioral Health

- When did you first observe these behaviors?
- When was the most recent occurrence of these behaviors, and what happened?

Once you have formed a thorough, accurate description of your concerns, consider what type of prevention (primary, secondary, or tertiary) and what type of mental-health provider you need to seek out. (We discuss types of mental-health professionals later in this chapter.) If you are a teacher, work with your administrators to determine how referrals work in your setting. If you are an administrator or another professional who helps develop these types of procedures, research what sorts of mental-health professionals are available in your area, what barriers to getting help are common for families, and what family-friendly methods exist for connecting children with beneficial services.

Step 3: The Intake Session

The first time a family meets with a mental-health provider is often called the intake session, clinical interview, or diagnostic interview. It usually lasts about one hour, and the family members should come prepared to discuss their child's and their family's medical, social, and legal history, such as parental custody arrangements or other guardianship set up through Child Protective Services, along with the reason or reasons why they are seeking an evaluation for their child.

During the intake session, family members learn about the provider's confidentiality practices and sign consent forms for the evaluation to take place. They can also sign release-of-information forms that will give the provider permission to talk to certain people about the child. (A sample release-of-information form appears in appendix B.) These people may include teachers, such as you, the child's pediatrician, or other caregivers. Without that signed consent, the provider cannot communicate with you about the child's evaluation. Additionally, if the child's parents are separated or divorced and share joint custody, both parents will have to consent to the evaluation and sign forms. However, they do not have to attend the intake session together if this is not in the best interests of the family.

Step 4: The Evaluation Period

At some point after the intake session, the provider meets directly with the child. This process typically involves an interview or conversation with the child, standardized assessments, and observations. It usually lasts several hours and may even occur over more than one day. Generally, the provider has the child's family members fill out questionnaires and also directly observes and interacts with the child. The provider may send out additional questionnaires for teachers or other caregivers to complete. The following table lists some common assessments and their uses.

INSTRUMENT	TOPIC	ADMINISTRATION METHOD
Autism Diagnostic Observation Schedule, Second Edition (ADOS-2)	Autism spectrum	Direct observation and interaction with provider
Bayley Scales of Infant and Toddler Development, Third Edition (Bayley-III)	Development	Direct observation and interaction with provider
Behavior Assessment System for Children, Third Edition (BASC-3)	Child behavior	Questionnaire for family members and teachers
Children's Apperception Test (CAT)	Projective (open-ended) task	Direct observation and interaction with provider
Children's Depression Inventory 2 (CDI 2)	Depression	Questionnaire for child
Child Behavior Checklist (CBCL)	Child behavior	Questionnaire for family members and teachers
Conners 3rd Edition (Conners 3)	ADHD	Questionnaire for family members and teachers
Kinetic Family Drawing	Projective (open-ended) drawing task	Direct observation and interaction with provider
NICHQ (National Institute for Children's Health Quality) Vanderbilt Assessment Scales	ADHD	Questionnaire for family members and teachers
Revised Children's Manifest Anxiety Scale, Second Edition (RCMAS-2)	Anxiety	Questionnaire for child

84

How Can I Help? A Teacher's Guide to Early Childhood Behavioral Health

INSTRUMENT	TOPIC	ADMINISTRATION METHOD
Sensory Profile-2	Sensory processing	Questionnaire for family members and teachers
Vineland Adaptive Behavior Scales-2	• Adaptive or self-help skills • Motor skills	• Questionnaire • Observation • Interview
Wechsler Intelligence Scale for Children, Fifth Edition (WISC-V)	Cognitive development	Direct observation and interaction with provider
Wechsler Preschool and Primary Scale of Intelligence, Fourth Edition (WPPSI-IV)	Cognitive development	Direct observation and interaction with provider

• •

Families sometimes engage in questionable "therapy"
that does not have good research support.
The California Evidence-Based Clearinghouse for Child Welfare
(**http://www.cebc4cw.org/search**), which provides descriptions
of treatments and interventions for young children,
can help you become familiar with what treatments
are and are not supported by research.

• •

Step 5: The Report and the Feedback Session

After the evaluation period, the evaluating provider creates a written report summarizing the evaluation process. This document usually includes a written history of the child and the important events and people in her life, any prior diagnoses or evaluations she has had, and a list of evaluation materials used in the current evaluation process. The report provides information on each assessment instrument used and gives an overall diagnosis (or diagnoses, in some cases), if one exists. Near the end of the report, the provider includes recommendations for family members, teachers, child-care facilities, or schools to help meet the child's needs.

When the report is ready, the family and the provider meet to review it, discuss the diagnosis or diagnoses and recommendations, and ask and answer additional questions. This meeting is often called a feedback session.

TYPES OF PROVIDERS
FOR YOUNG CHILDREN

Common providers in infant and early childhood mental health include
these professionals:

- Child psychiatrists

- Psychologists and counselors

- Social workers

- Child-development specialists and infant-mental-health (IMH) specialists

- Occupational therapists (OTs), physical therapists (PTs), and speech-language
  pathologists (SLPs)

These various titles can be confusing, so let's look at each profession more closely.
Some of these roles are closely related and therefore are covered in the same section.

Child Psychiatrists

A child psychiatrist is a physician who has completed medical school, holds a license
to practice medicine, and can diagnose children. She may work with children in a
medical setting, such as a hospital, physician's office, or health clinic, or have a private
practice. A child psychiatrist focuses on prescribing medication and monitoring children
who are taking it, so her appointments tend to be shorter than those of other mental-
health professionals. She may need to collect blood samples to monitor medication,
and she may use video chats and other communication technology to reach patients in
rural areas.

Psychologists and Counselors

A psychologist may work in a medical, school, or private-practice setting and can
conduct evaluations and therapy with children and their family members. She has a PhD
or a PsyD (doctor of psychology degree) and must have a license to practice in the state
where she works. Most states do not authorize psychologists to prescribe medication.
A counselor also provides therapy to children and their family members, generally
has completed a master's degree at a university, and holds a credential such as LPC
(Licensed Professional Counselor) or LMFT (Licensed Marriage and Family Therapist),
although other credentials are sometimes used. She can work for an agency that offers
mental-health services, in a hospital, or on her own in private practice.

Psychologists and counselors who provide therapy for children use techniques known as evidence-supported treatments (ESTs). The following chart contains some commonly used ESTs. *Evidence-supported* means that there is substantial research to support a given treatment.

TREATMENT	USED FOR	AGES OF PATIENTS	WEBSITE
Attachment and Biobehavioral Catch-Up (ABC)	Treating attachment or relational issues	6–48 months	http://www.abcintervention.org
Child-Parent Psychotherapy (CPP)	Treating trauma	0–5 years	https://www.nctsn.org/interventions/child-parent-psychotherapy
Cognitive behavioral therapy (CBT)	Changing thoughts	Preschool to adult	https://www.apa.org/ptsd-guideline/patients-and-families/cognitive-behavioral.aspx
Infant-Parent Psychotherapy (IPP)	Improving parent-child relationships	Birth to 3 years	https://sageclinic.org/infant-parent-psychotherapy-ipp
Eye Movement Desensitization and Reprocessing (EMDR)	Treating trauma	2 years and older	http://www.emdr.com/what-is-emdr
Parent-Child Interaction Therapy (PCIT)	• Changing children's behaviors • Improving caregiver-child relationships	2–7 years	http://www.cebc4cw.org/program/parent-child-interaction-therapy
Trauma-Focused Cognitive-Behavioral Therapy (TF-CBT)	Addressing thoughts and beliefs related to trauma	3 years and older	http://www.cebc4cw.org/program/trauma-focused-cognitive-behavioral-therapy

Social Workers

A social worker is sometimes also licensed as a counselor. She must have at least a bachelor's or master's degree to practice and often has the credentials BSW (Bachelor of Social Work), MSW (Master of Social Work), LMSW (Licensed Master of Social Work), or LCSW (Licensed Clinical Social Worker). She is often primarily concerned with the social conditions of a child's or family's life and in addressing social barriers that interfere with the child's or family's daily functioning, such as food insecurity or lack of transportation.

Child-Development Specialists and Infant-Mental-Health (IMH) Specialists

There is no national license for child-development specialists, so a given child-development specialist's job description may vary significantly from state to state.

She usually holds a master's degree (MA or MS) in child development, human development, or a similar field. She has studied typical development patterns in infants and children, aspects of atypical development, such as developmental disabilities or child maltreatment, and particularly the primary-caregiver-and-child relationship. A child-development specialist may work in early intervention, at a health department, or in a medical clinic; however, because she does not hold a national license, she probably does not have a private practice unless she has also completed licensure as a counselor or other therapist. Like an infant-mental-health (IMH) specialist, she focuses on early functioning and the importance of the relationships within a family.

Similarly, an IMH specialist does not hold a national license. However, many states have adopted credentials for these providers, so she may have a title such as Infant Mental Health Mentor, Level IV, Research (IMH-IV-R) or Infant Mental Health Specialist, Level III, Clinical (IMH-III-C) to indicate that she has completed certain training and practice experiences and is authorized to work with infant mental-health patients. An IMH

88

How Can I Help? A Teacher's Guide to Early Childhood Behavioral Health

specialist may work in home-based settings (visiting patients' homes to evaluate and treat them), in medical clinics, or in practices with other medical providers.

· ·

Healthy Steps is a developmental program that makes a child-development specialist available right in a pediatrician's office. This service is available throughout the United States and provides critical services, including developmental assessment, parenting consultations, and parenting support. Visit **www.healthysteps.org** for more information.

· ·

Occupational Therapists (OTs), Physical Therapists (PTs), and Speech-Language Pathologists (SLPs)

Occupational therapists (OTs), physical therapists (PTs), and speech-language pathologists (SLPs) all hold college degrees in their specialized fields and must be licensed to practice. An OT can work in a variety of independent-practice, school, and medical settings and helps patients address barriers that keep them from functioning at their best in their daily lives. She commonly helps children develop fine motor skills and may help them learn to better cope with sensory input. A PT also works with children to boost their physical abilities, but she focuses more on helping children improve their overall movement, endurance, and strength than on the activities of daily living. An SLP may also work in a variety of settings, including schools, private practice, or medical clinics. She helps children work on feeding, swallowing, literacy, and all aspects of communication.

CHAPTER 8:

Communicating and Working with Family Members

In any communications with family members about children's mental health—whether you are adding primary-prevention information to your weekly emails or updating specific family members on your efforts to implement their child's individualized education program (IEP)—understanding your audience is key. Family members have widely varying levels of education and past experience and sometimes even have mental-health challenges themselves. Your objectives are to communicate important information about each child to his family members in a way that the family members *can* hear and understand it, not merely in the way that you *want* them to hear it, and to work with each child's family members to meet his unique needs. These goals require both general and individualized efforts.

TIPS FOR GENERAL COMMUNICATION

Your General Communication Plan

Every teacher needs a general plan for communicating year-round with all family members. That plan should include regular information about broad mental-health and well-being topics, chosen based on the ages of the children you work with and the needs of their families and the community. You can easily provide this information through both traditional and contemporary communication methods.

SAMPLE TRADITIONAL COMMUNICATION METHODS	SAMPLE CONTEMPORARY COMMUNICATION METHODS
Newsletters Bulletin boards In-person meetings Family-night events	Emails Facebook Twitter YouTube Other social-media platforms

Use multiple forms of both types of communication to meet all families where they are. It can be extremely helpful to have all families fill out a survey of their preferred communication methods. When planning a year of family education, also plan the communication methods you will use for each topic. For example, you might decide to use a newsletter and a Facebook post to share information about one topic and to use an email, a family-night event, and a post on your program's website to share information about another topic. Here is a sample schedule of communications for an infant-and-toddler program:

- August or beginning of school year: helping a child adjust to child care

- Beginning of school year: typical progression of separation anxiety

- Late summer or early fall: infant sleep (sleep needs, safe sleep, sleep hygiene)

- Early in school year: how to quickly respond to a baby's cries and offer comfort

- Fall: secure-base phenomenon (how to support children as they explore and return to school)

- Fall and winter: handling holiday stress (behavior guidance, calming techniques)

- Timed for each child: developmental information for babies at six, eight, ten, and twelve months old

- Various times:

  » Helping a baby at the doctor (for example, methods to comfort and distract a baby for immunizations)

  » Taking the fight out of mealtimes (desirable mealtime routines, how to structure meals)

  » Helping a child adjust to a new baby (tips on handling adjustment and behavioral regression)

  » How to stop saying "no" all the time (positive behavior guidance)

  » Typical progression of stranger anxiety

This type of regular communication helps get quality information about typical development into the hands of all family members. This is primary prevention in action, and it helps build strong foundations for healthy family member–child relationships. As you learn more about children and their family members, you will discover overall patterns and individual preferences that can suggest ways to improve your communications, whether in general or with a specific person. For instance, you might need to simplify the vocabulary in your messages because many family members are English language learners, or you might need to provide hard copies of your electronic newsletters to a certain family member because he does not have internet access at home.

Teacher Task #1: Your Communication Preferences

To communicate effectively with the family members of all your students, you will probably need to get out of your comfort zone and communicate in more ways than you usually do. For instance, not all family members check their email regularly, text, or use social media, so you will not reach everyone if you rely solely on these channels.

Use this chart to help you determine your natural communication preferences and your potential areas for growth in communication. For each communication method, mark the column that best describes how you feel about using that method.

COMMUNICATION METHOD	I PREFER USING THIS METHOD.	I WOULD LIKE TO BE GOOD AT USING THIS METHOD.	I AVOID USING THIS METHOD.
Speaking to a large group			
Leading icebreaker activities			
Writing a blog post			
Posting to social media, such as Facebook or Twitter			
Making printed newsletters			
Writing email newsletters			

COMMUNICATION METHOD	I PREFER USING THIS METHOD.	I WOULD LIKE TO BE GOOD AT USING THIS METHOD.	I AVOID USING THIS METHOD.
Sending reminders through text messages			
Hand-writing notes			
Making a bulletin board for adults			
Other (specify):			

Tips for Difficult Conversations

As any experienced teacher knows, general communication cannot prevent all problems. Sometimes you will need to have difficult conversations with family members to do what is best for a child. Following these rules can help you handle these tricky encounters.

Rule 1: Respect Confidentiality

Avoid bringing up sensitive information within earshot of others or putting it in an email. (Your program or school may have policies prohibiting these actions.) A difficult conversation will go more smoothly if you hold it privately and at a time when the family member is not rushed.

Rule 2: Respect the Family Member's Expertise

Address the family member as the expert on his child. If you begin a conversation by giving advice, the family member may feel attacked or talked down to and become defensive:

>> **Teacher:** I think you should help Terrell get to bed earlier.

>> **Family member:** What? Are you saying I let him stay up too late? Who are you to tell me how to raise my own kid?

94

How Can I Help? A Teacher's Guide to Early Childhood Behavioral Health

Defensive family members will probably not be open to suggestions, even research-based, well-intentioned ones. Instead, before you offer advice, express genuine concern and ask sincere questions. Remember, the family member has most likely known the child longer than you have and has rich information about how the child functions outside of school:

> » **Teacher:** I've noticed that Terrell rubs his eyes a lot during the day and seems to get irritated easily. I'm wondering what you've noticed.

> » **Family member:** Well, his bedtime is 8:30, and I . . .

Rule 3: Communicate Good Things Too

How would you feel if you had a friend who only talked to or texted you to criticize or whine about something? You probably would avoid him, block his number, end the friendship, or all three. Family members have similar feelings when you contact them solely to report problems with their child. Avoid communicating only when a child has had a "bad" day or when there is a complaint. Build a relationship with each child's family member in which you communicate regularly about the good and the bad in your interactions with that child.

One way to regularly communicate about good things is to send written daily reports to family members to highlight their children's activities. These types of records are intended to help a family picture their child's day, not to create a list of things for which he should be punished or to qualitatively rate how he "performed." To family members, a written record of negatives can feel like a traffic ticket at the end of a long day, so if you do need to communicate something negative, wait until you can speak with the family member. Instead, focus your written reports on what the child enjoyed and accomplished that day. Even hearing about small things—such as how a child loved playing in the sensory table, enjoyed the fruit at snack time, or laughed at the geese he saw on a walk—can light up a family member's day!

Rule 4: Use Positive Bookends

When you must deliver a negative message to a child's family members, bookend that message by stating two positive things about the child's day: one before you mention the problem and one after. This practice helps combat the idea that a child's whole day was either "bad" or "good." All days—for children and for adults—include both good and bad. The positive ending comment is especially helpful because a family member may feel discouraged after hearing about his child's negative behavior. The fact that you still see something positive in the child can give the family member a message of hope.

Rule 5: Avoid Unintentional Ambushes

Collecting data on behaviors and symptoms can provide valuable information to help you assist a child. However, telling a family member, "I've been tracking your child's behavior for a while, and . . ." can start the conversation off on an adversarial foot. No one wants to feel blindsided by a sudden flood of negative information. Changing your language a bit to something such as, "I've noticed that each day after lunch . . ." can make a big difference.

Rule 6: Clearly State Your Actions and Expectations

When you inform a family member of a child's negative behavior in your classroom, the family member often feels obligated to punish the child at home in response to your complaint. However, this step can actually make classroom behaviors worse because the family member's efforts will be too far removed from the incident for the child to understand the connection between his behavior and the punishment. Instead, the child may feel angry or sad over the seemingly random penalty, carry those feelings back to your classroom with him, and express them by continuing to act out.

To prevent these spiraling consequences, during the conversation with the family member about the original behavior, make sure to clearly explain what happened and what you have already done to address the behavior. Emphasize that the goal of this discussion is to inform the family member of the incident and to learn about ways that you can help the child; you are not trying to get the family member to further punish the child. For example, you might say something like this: "Lamont screamed and pulled out a chunk of his own hair during the transition to nap time today. I took him to the calming area, showed him how to use a fidget to keep his hands busy, and stayed with him until he calmed down." Let the family member know that you do not expect him to address the incident with the child at home. However, you can ask if anything similar has occurred previously and, if so, how the family member addressed it.

Teacher Task #2: Planning for a Difficult Conversation

Imagine that a child in your care is having extreme difficulty separating from a family member at drop-off each day. Despite your best efforts, the child always cries for thirty

96

How Can I Help? A Teacher's Guide to Early Childhood Behavioral Health

minutes or more after the family member leaves. How would you have a conversation with the family member about this behavior? Consider these elements:

- Timing your approach
- Opening with positive comments and feedback
- Describing the behavior you have observed and your response
- Explaining the results you want from this conversation
- Closing with positive comments to provide a message of hope

Refining Your Communication Skills

Sometimes you can follow all the tips we have discussed for good communication but still find that your message just does not seem to land in the way you would like. When this happens, start by consulting with a trusted colleague. You might want to role-play a conversation together and videotape it if you can. What details do you and your colleague notice about your voice, gestures, body language, and facial expressions? Sometimes we simply do not recognize our own subtle practices that impede good communication.

In some cases, communication difficulties have nothing to do with you. A family member's personal history and experiences (including any history of trauma), relationship with your program, pattern of substance abuse (if any), personality factors, educational level, and culture can all cause communication barriers. When developing a plan for improving communication with a given family member, focus on adjusting factors within your control, such as the reading level of your weekly newsletter, your attempts at building rapport, and the level of cultural sensitivity and responsiveness in your classroom.

WORKING WITH FAMILY MEMBERS WHO HAVE MENTAL-HEALTH CHALLENGES

Sometimes you may have difficulty communicating with a family member because he himself has a mental-health challenge. Many of the disorders discussed in this book can affect adults as well as children. This section includes some additional mental-health concerns that commonly or exclusively affect adults: personality disorders and mood disorders.

What Is a Personality Disorder?

Personality is a pattern of behavior that reflects a person's internal experience of the world and himself. The DSM-5 explains that when this pattern is markedly different from typical development, causes impaired functioning, or creates distress (or involves some combination of these results) *and* is rigidly expressed, this "personality" may actually be a personality disorder. The patterns of a personality disorder usually emerge in late adolescence or in early adulthood; young children are never diagnosed with personality disorders.

The DSM-5 estimates that only about 15 percent of adults have a personality disorder, so most family members you encounter will not present the challenges described in the rest of this section. However, by understanding the traits of some of these disorders, you can tailor your communication to family members who do have them so that that information can ultimately benefit their children.

Cluster A Personality Disorders

Personality disorders are grouped into three categories. The first type, Cluster A, includes personality disorders in which family members may appear odd or paranoid. A highly social or outgoing teacher may have trouble communicating with family members who have Cluster A disorders, because these family members will rarely engage in communications. Let go of the expectation that you will "fix" anyone, and instead focus on getting information into family members' hands. If one channel does not work, try others. For example, if a family member will not give you his email address, you can put information from your emails on a bulletin board in your classroom. If he does not want to engage with your program's social-media platforms, such as by joining a Facebook group or following a blog, you can send home a paper newsletter. You might not make friends with these kinds of family members—and that is okay—but you must be reliable, predictable, and nonjudgmental when communicating with them.

Paranoid Personality Disorder

A family member who expresses paranoia may have a realistic basis for doing so; for example, if authority figures have deceived or targeted him before, it is reasonable to expect that he would be cautious when dealing with them again. However, when an individual with paranoid personality disorder shows suspicion, avoids confiding in others, feels attacked or judged, or is unforgiving, these behaviors may not necessarily

98

How Can I Help? A Teacher's Guide to Early Childhood Behavioral Health

be rooted in experience or objective fact. A family member with paranoid personality disorder may be unreasonably suspicious of your inquiries about his child, may avoid communications with you, or may see neutral behavior from you, such as saying, "I haven't seen you lately," as a judgment or insult.

To maximize effective communication with a family member who has this disorder, remember that the paranoia is not actually about you, the teacher. Honestly answer the family member's questions about confidentiality, video or audio recordings that might be made in the classroom, such as on security cameras, and the use of photos taken in the classroom. Be patient, as paranoia is not easily allayed and you will have to repeatedly reassure this family member. He may be sensitive to subtle changes, such as having his newsletter printed on a different color paper than someone else's. Be consistent with communication formats to avoid the appearance of singling this family member out.

Schizoid Personality Disorder

Individuals with schizoid personality disorder may not enjoy socializing, close friendships, or intimate relationships. They generally prefer to be alone and may not appear emotionally expressive. As a result, they have little desire to get to know teachers on a personal level and are unlikely to be attracted to classroom social activities, such as family-night get-togethers.

To communicate successfully with a family member who has this disorder, provide accurate information about classroom activities in ways that do not require socializing. For instance, try sending an email or a note instead of having a conversation with the family member at pick-up time. If your program hosts a family-member night, send the notes from your presentation to all family members afterwards.

Schizotypal Personality Disorder

If a family member has schizotypal personality disorder, he may appear odd or unusual in his appearance or his thinking, such as having magical beliefs or superstitious practices. He may seem paranoid or anxious and may have trouble establishing or even desiring close relationships.

Remember that communication must happen regardless of a family member's appearance or beliefs. You do not have to condone his behavior or choices to keep him informed about his child's well-being. Family members also more willingly engage in communication when they do not feel judged.

Cluster B Personality Disorders

Family members with Cluster B personality disorders tend to be highly emotional and dramatic and can be puzzling to work with. There is a good bit of variation among Cluster B disorders, but the defining characteristic of this type of disorder is problems with self-control and regulating emotions.

Antisocial Personality Disorder

Family members with antisocial personality disorder may have histories of criminal behavior and typically act only for themselves, without much concern for the well-being of others. They frequently engage in deceitful practices, are impulsive and reckless, tend to get into physical altercations, and can be highly physically and verbally aggressive. They demonstrate little regard for safety, legal, or social norms and tend to have histories of financial, employment, and relationship instability.

A family member with this disorder is often more distantly than directly involved with his child. On the other hand, when such a family member is actively parenting, he may dismiss or challenge your authority. He might also disregard program rules, such as attendance, payment, or health-care guidelines.

When communicating with a family member who has antisocial personality disorder, remember that puffing yourself up to be the "bigger" authority will not work. People with this disorder simply do not care about authority. Their behaviors will escalate, and because your job is to keep yourself, your colleagues, and the children safe, you need to avoid altercations. Let go of the expectation that this family member will care about or respect your authority.

Make your program's rules clear to all families, but remember that this family member is highly likely to violate rules. Be sure that you have systemic support from your program to enforce rules, such as procedures for late arrivals, so that the family member does not

100

How Can I Help? A Teacher's Guide to Early Childhood Behavioral Health

identify one person as the "hard" person or the "easy" person and does not think that he can get away with inappropriate behavior just because a certain staff member is present or absent. Again, consistency is key.

Borderline Personality Disorder (BPD)

A family member with borderline personality disorder (BPD) may immediately seem to cling to you, offering praise, compliments, and even friendship. However, this type of relationship is fragile and can quickly turn into a neediness that you simply cannot fulfill as a teacher. Relationship problems are the hallmark of BPD, and family members with this disorder may be moody and impulsive, change relationships often, and even attempt self-harm or suicide.

Good boundaries are the key to working with a family member with BPD. As teachers, we often have a need to help that can sometimes cause us to violate boundaries. To avoid doing this, stay up to date on your program's policies, especially about resources and their availability. For instance, does your school or center have a bus-ticket program, clothing vouchers, or a food pantry that is available to students' family members? Having a list of resources and backup resources can help you be prepared when a family member comes to you and asks for a ride, food, or money. All teachers have probably opened up the school food pantry "just this once" for a family member who needed something. Typically, that "just this once" is indeed just one time; when it comes to a person with BPD, however, one time is never enough. The requests will keep coming and will get increasingly demanding, and eventually you will let the person down.

Histrionic Personality Disorder and Narcissistic Personality Disorder

Individuals with histrionic personality disorder or narcissistic personality disorder tend to prefer to have the focus of a group on themselves. While individuals with histrionic personality disorder may come across as sexualized and dramatic, individuals with narcissistic personality disorder tend to feel that they are entitled or special compared to others. People with either disorder seek out attention; individuals with histrionic personality disorder may erroneously perceive that they have a special bond with a teacher.

Family members with either of these disorders will more likely respond to information that clearly applies to them than to information that is sent solely for the benefit of their children. For instance, if you are sending out information about a family-member meeting, mention to these individuals that this meeting includes free child care and an opportunity to socialize. If you are creating a social-media post about putting children to bed on time, also include information about how this practice will benefit family members, such as having more time to themselves in the evening and not having to deal with grumpy children the next day.

Cluster C Personality Disorders

The final group of personality disorders, Cluster C, consists of certain disorders that all have anxious behaviors in common:

- Family members with avoidant disorders may view themselves as much less competent than you view them, and they may take vague comments about "people" as being about themselves. For example, if a teacher complains of hating "people who are always late," a family member with an avoidant disorder may perceive this statement as a veiled criticism of him.

- Family members with dependent disorders may come to lean on you for parent-like approval and praise. They frequently volunteer to help in the classroom but may need exceptional amounts of instruction and reinforcement.

- Family members with obsessive-compulsive personality disorder (OCPD) use perfectionism to cope with their anxiety (even though this practice actually gets in the way of completing a task) and may be rigid about policies, procedures, and minute details. These family members may be unwilling to go along with others' plans because they do not want to lose control of a situation.

Communicating with family members who have Cluster C disorders means being patient with a whole spectrum of needs for control, reinforcement, and reassurance. Although anxiety may take a different form for each disorder, it remains the common thread among all of them, and it means that a teacher must maintain consistent communication, be conscientious about keeping promises, and be flexible in terms of control and oversight when taking on volunteers.

Mood Disorders

Among family members, more common than personality disorders are mood disorders, such as anxiety or depression. Though we have already discussed how these conditions affect young children, these disorders look different for adults.

Anxiety Disorders

The most common anxiety disorders for adults are social anxiety disorder, in which anxiety is specifically tied to social situations; and generalized anxiety disorder (GAD), in

102

How Can I Help? A Teacher's Guide to Early Childhood Behavioral Health

which anxiety is more pervasive across settings and situations. These and other anxiety disorders cause frequent out-of-control worry and physical agitation that disrupt the individual's life.

When you speak with a family member who has social anxiety disorder, he may be preoccupied with his own anxiety and may not actually process the information that you deliver verbally. In cases like these, you may want to also provide the information in writing so that the family member does not have to process the stress of a social interaction along with the memory demands of remembering what you say. Likewise, some family members with anxiety disorders simply cannot or will not attend a large-group meeting, so make sure to have the information from these meetings available in other formats (such by putting it in a newsletter or by having one-on-one conversations with these family members).

It is good practice to be clear about your expectations when working with any family member, but it is even more important when working with family members who have anxiety disorders. Brainstorm ahead of time about what concerns family members might have regarding a given situation. For example, if there is a family-member meeting, what is the dress code? What should family members bring? Are children, including children who do not attend the school or program, allowed? Will there be food? For family-member conferences, what are the start and end times? Be exceptionally clear with your information and expectations, as this information will help lower anxiety for family members.

Depressive Disorders

Depressive disorders in adults include, but are not limited to, major depressive disorder (MDD) and persistent depressive disorder. Both of these disorders cause feelings of sadness or hopelessness, loss of interest in life's activities, changes in weight gain and sleep, low energy, problems with clarity of thought or concentration, thoughts of death, or some combination of these difficulties. Symptoms may persist from two weeks to more than two years. A family member with a depressive disorder will often struggle with remembering his commitments, participating in the classroom, and following through on activities that require energy. He may struggle with motivation because even though he wants to be involved, the disorder dampens his ability to engage.

When working with family members who have depressive disorders, provide frequent reminders to assist with memory or attention problems. Depressive disorders are draining and can keep people from completing tasks even if they want to do them, so be prepared in case a family member cannot complete volunteer assignments. Provide reinforcement for small progress, and avoid punitive or humiliating remarks or comparing the family member to others.

Set appropriate boundaries; you do not need to "parent" family members or provide therapy to them. But as a teacher, you can encourage them to seek help by explaining how depressive symptoms can interfere with their efforts to do what is best for their children and their children's education. Encourage family members to connect with supportive people or groups. As always, if you suspect child abuse or neglect, report it.

HOW CAN I BE NONJUDGMENTAL WHEN I FEEL SO JUDGMENTAL?

Because family members with mental-health challenges can behave in ways that we may view as unconventional or even bizarre, we can easily slip into being judgmental of them. In fact, all humans do this, all the time. We do it when we hear someone's explanation for being late or when we listen to a story about what a coworker did over the weekend. We mentally compare ourselves to others ("Not what I would have done!"), or we decide whether a person is giving a valid reason or merely an excuse.

Note that sometimes *making judgments* is necessary for our own and others' protection, such as if a child comes to school with a mysterious injury or if a family member repeatedly misses payment due dates despite numerous reminders. But *being judgmental*, or thinking unnecessarily critically of someone based on our own views about his behavior, typically does not help us communicate effectively with family members, particularly family members who have mental-health challenges. So how do we become less judgmental in our interactions with family members?

The first step is not to let go of our every instinct and opinion; instead, it is to recognize when we are being judgmental. For instance, when a family member arrives late for pick-up for the fourth time in two weeks, we probably already have critical thoughts

104

How Can I Help? A Teacher's Guide to Early Childhood Behavioral Health

about why it happened, based on what we know about him ("He forgot to get gas *again*, didn't he?"). These judgmental thoughts eat at our energy, and during conversations, they can keep us from really listening to what a family member has to say. The next time you find yourself thinking about your response to a family member before that person has even opened his mouth, try this:

1. Take deep belly breaths. This involves more than filling your chest with air. Breathe so deeply that your stomach pushes out with each inhale and moves back in with each exhale.

2. Tell yourself, "My judgment is not needed yet; I push it to the side."

3. After the conversation, refocus yourself by asking, "What is the important thing about this interaction for the *child*?"

Of course, your judgmental self will try to resurface throughout this process. As that happens, practice separating your judgmental thoughts, feelings, and actions from those that are in the best interests of the child.

For instance, imagine that Roberto, who tends to get soaked while playing at the water table, once again has no spare clothes at school. You have reminded his family members repeatedly, but they still have not brought any more clothes in. You are feeling frustrated and angry. "Can't they be responsible? I bet they don't even care," you say to yourself. You can sense the tension in your face and body.

This is the time to separate your thoughts. Take a deep breath and ask yourself, "What does *Roberto* need?" Spare clothes. Anything else? "To feel cared for at school." Those are your actions: get the spare clothes, and make sure that Roberto's needs are met when he is with you. Even if his family members are indeed irresponsible and uncaring (which you cannot know for sure anyway, as you do not know everything), you cannot change them, nor is it your job to do so.

Remember to avoid sharing your negative thoughts and feelings about family members with children. The desire to share those thoughts comes from your judgmental self—the part you do not need right now. Bad-mouthing a family member to a child will not make the spare clothes appear (or solve whatever the issue is), and it can leave the child feeling conflicted because of the discord he sees between adults whom he values. Wait to vent until you have a private moment with a trusted friend or colleague. For now, focus on your top priority: caring for the child.

CHAPTER 9:

Successful Coping
and Self-Care for Teachers

Self-care may be one of the most misused phrases in today's world, used to justify everything from overeating to overspending to just-plain-poor choices. The good news is that self-care—genuine self-care—is critical, so you as a teacher may give yourself permission to make it a habit. The not-so-good news is that good self-care requires that you engage in it on purpose, and that means planning, organizing, and prioritizing one more thing in your life. However, once taking care of yourself in meaningful ways becomes a habit, it can bring you lifelong benefits. Here are some small ways, and a few big ones, to slip better self-nurturance into your life.

GET ENOUGH QUALITY SLEEP

There is a good reason that sleep is number one on our list of self-care items. Getting your eight hours is critically important. (By the way, that means eight hours of sleep, not three hours of Netflix in bed and then five hours of sleep.)

How much sleep do you think you get, on average, a night? Teachers cannot physically go without regular sleep and hope to "catch up" on the weekends; sleep researcher Daniel Cohen and his colleagues tell us that it is not possible. Just as the children in your care need good sleep, you do, too. Without it, as you have undoubtedly experienced, you suffer the consequences: depressed or irritable mood, wandering attention, and so on.

However, sometimes the issue is not the quantity of your sleep but the quality. Good sleep hygiene starts before you actually get into bed. Think about your bedroom. How many of these criteria for good sleep can you check off?

- I keep my room dark and cool for sleeping.

- I stop using electronic devices thirty minutes before bed.

- I cannot see lights from chargers, televisions, or other electronics from my bed.

- I feel safe in the room where I sleep.

- I go to bed and get up at about the same time every day.

- If I wake up in the middle of the night, I avoid turning on an electronic device to play games or check email.

- I monitor and limit my daily caffeine use.

Once you actually get into bed and lie down, it can help to focus on your breathing, taking deep, slow breaths in and out. As you breathe in, let the air push your stomach out; as you breathe out, let your stomach flatten. Remember to breathe all the way from your stomach and not just from your chest. As you inhale, imagine that calm, cool air is moving through your body and sweeping through your head, torso, and limbs successively like a wave. Imagine that it takes with it any pain, tightness, or worry that it touches. Allow the cool air to hold onto the negative thoughts and feelings in your body, and visualize those elements exiting your body as you exhale. Repeat this exercise several times.

Quieting Your Mind

Even if you practice good sleep hygiene, your body will keep you awake on some nights because of pain, hormones, or other causes. However, your mind may be the most frequent culprit that prevents you from getting in a good night of sleep. Therefore, mastering your thoughts is another important step in quality sleep. These three techniques can help you accomplish this task; you can also use them throughout your day to manage stress.

Focus on the Positive

Try to plant positive thoughts and imagery in your mind before you head to bed. Each night, take a few minutes to write down five things for which you are grateful. These can be big things, such as life, faith, family, health, and home; little things, such as the taste of your favorite tea, the scent of roses in your flowerbeds, or the way it feels to laugh with your best friend; or some of each. Let go of any end-of-the-day anger that keeps you from acknowledging that you have things to be grateful for.

To learn more about living gratefully, try reading the book *Simple Abundance: A Daybook of Comfort and Joy* by Sarah Breathnach.

Write Down Your Lists

Teachers are notorious for having endless lists, and these tend to come alive just when our bodies are ready for sleep. But to lie in bed at night and attempt to mentally hold onto a list virtually poisons any chance for peaceful sleep. To manage these disruptive thoughts, try keeping paper and a pen by your bed. When nagging thoughts arise, anything from "remember to send the permission slips home tomorrow" to "get milk at the grocery store," jot them down. Do it quickly and without a lot of extra writing. It is better to take a few seconds to get these thoughts out of your head than to try to remember them all night!

Dismiss and Replace Distressing Thoughts

Avoid imagining conversations or conflicts or reviewing actual ones from your day while you are trying to go to sleep. Anything that has you thinking, "I should have said . . . ," or "I should have done . . ." is taking you down the wrong path. Learn to notice when your thoughts turn to real or imagined conflict or drama, and pay attention to how these stressful contemplations begin to take a toll on your body through increased heart rate, perspiration, or muscle tension.

Once you recognize that this process is happening, engage in thought stopping, replacement, and visualization. Identify which thoughts are bringing you distress instead of relaxation. Then mentally stop them by acknowledging that you are having distressing thoughts, telling yourself that it is time to change those thoughts, *and replacing them*. Replacing is key because trying *not* to think about something actually leads to more thinking about that thing. (For example, if you try *not* to think about chocolate cake, how well does it work?) It undoes all your purposeful relaxation!

To create a go-to replacement for negative thoughts, find or create an image or scenario that relaxes you. Many people enjoy picturing themselves in nature, but any calming

109

Chapter 9: Successful Coping and Self-Care for Teachers

image will do. Then visualize yourself in that image or scenario, vividly imagining what you can see, hear, smell, taste, and feel.

PROGRESSIVE MUSCLE RELAXATION

Another useful technique for stress management is progressive muscle relaxation. For instance, notice where your shoulders are right now. Are they relaxed, or are they tensed and raised? Take a moment to raise them high up by your ears and hold them there. Now let them down. Do they feel lower than before? In the middle of a busy day or a tense situation, combine this tense-and-relax exercise with a few deep breaths.

When you have more time, you can also try tensing and relaxing different muscle groups progressively throughout your body. Get in the habit of checking on yourself throughout the workday to see whether you are managing your stress.

MEDITATE

Your mind works overtime trying to keep up with everything you need to do and remember. It needs sleep to help organize and manage all this information. However, meditation can offer some of the same brain benefits without requiring you to take a full nap. Note that sufficient sleep is still required for overall health.

Meditation can seem intimidating, but you can start small. Find a comfortable place where you can sit without interruption for a few minutes. Close your eyes and commit to focusing on your breathing for five minutes. (If you are brand-new to meditation, set a timer.) As thoughts pop into your head—and they will—imagine gently blowing them out of your mind with your breathing. For five minutes, your mind needs to do nothing but be aware of how you are breathing in and out. If five minutes is too much at first, try three or even one! Meditation takes practice.

110

How Can I Help? A Teacher's Guide to Early Childhood Behavioral Health

See these websites for more information about
mindfulness and meditation:

https://www.mayoclinic.org/healthy-lifestyle/consumer-health/
in-depth/mindfulness-exercises/art-20046356

https://www.theatlantic.com/education/archive/2015/08/
mindfulness-education-schools-meditation/402469/

https://www.gaiam.com/blogs/discover/meditation-101-
techniques-benefits-and-a-beginner-s-how-to

LIMIT CLUTTER

Look around you. Clutter tends to follow us from work to our cars to our homes, but this phenomenon does not help our mental health. When we are in our homes, even in our beds, and are surrounded by piles of papers, laundry, and other objects, we do not feel rested. At best, we have a nagging sense that we need to get up and clean. At worst, we find ourselves sitting in anger and distraction, unable to meet our other obligations or take the mental breaks we deserve.

Still, limiting clutter can be tough for teachers. You know how to recycle and save objects, and you know the value in having a box of paper-towel tubes available when you need them (and sometimes you do need them). Teachers are not wasters, and this means that sometimes you live with a lot of extra "stuff" without having a lot of extra storage space. From a practical standpoint, we must all find a balance between having functional spaces and saving useful or recyclable items. Sometimes finding that balance means donating or sharing some of our resources.

BE IN THE MOMENT

At moments when you feel overwhelmed, reduce your thinking to the smallest possible unit of time. For example, imagine yourself in group time, trying to read a story aloud. The children are fidgety and talkative, and your mind starts to wander to what will happen if the lunch cart arrives late and throws off your schedule for the rest of the afternoon. You begin to feel annoyed at the thought that lunch, nap time, and your whole day could fall apart. You start mentally blaming the kitchen staff for not getting the cart here on time, and your irritation grows.

At this point, your mind is not where your body is: it is away from your present, engaging in worry. In this type of situation, when you become overwhelmed with thoughts about the future, pull yourself back to immediacy by taking a deep, cleansing breath and asking yourself, "For the next five seconds, where do I need to be and what do I need to be doing?" The likely answer for this scenario? "I need to be here, engaging these children in a fun story."

When you focus on the current moment, you can release thoughts about anything beyond the next five seconds and instead concentrate on what you need to do here and now. In our example, those responsibilities include showing pictures, using a dramatic reading voice and facial expressions to engage the children, and connecting with them. Being irritated about the lunch cart will not make it arrive sooner, but dwelling on this future, out-of-your-control element can make you act more irritable during story time than you would like to.

EXAMINE YOUR CIRCLE OF CONTROL

When we give in to our emotions, we often lose our sense of what we can and cannot control. Both children and adults can benefit from this simple perspective-restoring exercise:

1. Draw a large circle on a piece of paper. Leave enough room to write both inside and outside the circle. This your circle of control.

2. Inside the circle, write down all your concerns that you *can* control, such as putting gas in your car, managing your temper, or setting your alarm and packing your lunch for tomorrow morning.

3. Outside the circle, write down all your concerns that you *cannot* control, such as how much an upcoming medical bill might be, whether a child's family member likes you, or what the weather will be for your family picnic on Saturday.

All the items inside your circle of control are issues that you can manage by taking concrete steps. To reduce your concerns about these items, take the necessary steps, such as setting a reminder on your phone to fill up on gas when you leave work. In contrast, you cannot do anything to change the items outside your circle of control, so

112

How Can I Help? A Teacher's Guide to Early Childhood Behavioral Health

dwelling on them can lead to unnecessary worry and stress. Focus on taking care of what's in your circle, and deal with the issues outside your circle as they come.

SET A TIMER

We all sometimes put off big tasks until the last minute because they seem so overwhelming that we just cannot get started. However, just because a task is big does not mean that you have to complete it all in one sitting. Maybe you cannot spend an hour right now working on children's portfolios, but can you work for ten minutes? Maybe you want to create an office space at home, but organizing that entire part of the house seems like too much. Instead, can you spend fifteen minutes working on one box? Mentally, it is very helpful and motivating to go from thinking that a task will take "forever" to putting a firm limit on how long we will let it take on any particular day.

CHECK FOR COGNITIVE DISTORTIONS

We all tend to develop certain bad habits when it comes to thinking about our lives, work, and problems. Dwelling on dysfunctional or unproductive thoughts gets in the way of our abilities to function and meet our goals. Mental-health professionals refer to these bad thinking habits as *cognitive distortions*. See which of these common cognitive distortions you can identify with:

- **Blaming:** When we do not perform as we wish, we blame others. This can sound like, "I wouldn't have been late if traffic hadn't been so bad," or "I had that paper right in my hand, but then Ms. Campbell started griping at me and made me forget where I put it." But are these things really someone else's fault?

- **Mind-reading:** We "just know" (whether or not we have any evidence) what someone else is going to say or how she will react to us: "If I say anything to Ms. Hu about Zhong's behavior today, she'll freak out and start accusing me." So we either gear up for a fight or do not even bother to have a conversation.

- **Discounting the good:** Have you ever noticed that one bad thing can overshadow a whole day of good things? This cognitive distortion often includes the words, "Yes, but . . ." For example, a colleague might say, "I think today went really well," and we might respond, "Yes, but Emilia just *had* to bite Jaden and ruin circle time!" Sometimes one unpleasant experience can blind us to all the other good things happening in our lives.

- **Catastrophizing:** We lose perspective and blow an unpleasant event out of proportion. Does a child having a temper tantrum at drop-off really make a disaster of the entire day?

CHECK YOUR RELATIONSHIPS

As researchers Melissa Nachmias and her colleagues demonstrate, a child manages stress better when she has a secure attachment relationship. This phenomenon also has implications for adults. Our early attachment relationships are always with us, influencing our current abilities to manage, establish, and make use of our relationships. Who are your trustworthy people? Which people in your life provide support, encouragement, and nurturance, and which people bring conflict and distress? Use the answers to these questions to make changes in your relationships so that they support you rather than drain you.

For an excellent review of attachment and stress, visit **https://cehdvision2020.umn. edu/blog/secure-attachment-relationships**

HAVE SOMETHING TO LOOK FORWARD TO

What is the last thing you looked forward to? Was it something big, such as a day off, a vacation, or a major purchase? Milestones matter in our lives, and we should enjoy the important memories they make. But for most of us, these major events simply do not come along often enough! You would not go a week without eating just so you could enjoy one meal or go a month without sleeping just so you could enjoy one nap. Your emotional health should not depend on few-and-far-between events, either.

Instead of focusing solely on big rewards or vacations, think about the concepts of pleasure, joy, and peace. Now think about finding moments of those emotions in your life every day. Yes, every day! For most of us, that is an incredible goal in our stress-filled lives, and we can only achieve it by working purposefully on it.

Teacher Task #1: Your Simple Joys

The first step in finding daily pleasure, joy, and peace is to spend some time reflecting on what brings you those emotions. For example, I made this list of simple activities that bring me joy:

- Eating dark chocolate
- Playing a game on my phone

114

How Can I Help? A Teacher's Guide to Early Childhood Behavioral Health

- Watching my favorite TV show

- Looking at memes online

- Planning for Christmas

- Organizing art supplies

- Making quilt squares

- Drinking chai

- Scrapbooking

- Meeting friends for coffee

Now make your own list of activities that bring you pleasure, joy, or peace. How many of these do you think you could schedule into your life in the next week?

Guidelines for Scheduled Joy

As you implement scheduled joy (or pleasure or peace) into your life, remember these guidelines:

- Avoid making plans that depend entirely on other people or their schedules. Do not forego something you want and need just because someone else cancels.

- The simpler the plan, the better. Allowing yourself to savor one delicious chocolate in silence and solitude before leaving school is much more achievable than getting a sitter for your own children, buying supplies, and making chocolate. You can find satisfaction in this big endeavor, but it is harder to pull off because it requires involving other people, having money available, and having leftover energy at the end of the day.

- Time matters, but so does quality. It might take only five minutes to play a word game or enjoy a few sips of tea, but that time only counts as self-care if it is devoted solely to your self-care activity. No multitasking allowed!

- Start low and slow. Most of us do not have time for sixty straight minutes of TV or other self-care every night, but we can sneak in five or ten minutes here and there to pay attention to ourselves. Avoid setting yourself up for failure by over-scheduling your time. Can you secure one hour a week for yourself? If so, great! If not, decide on the smallest unit of meaningful self-care you need and seek for that. For instance, taking an hour a week for a massage is wishful thinking for most of us, but setting aside ten minutes for meditation before bed each night is more achievable (and can be more powerful).

- It may work better to combat stress in small increments throughout the day than to save everything up for the end. Can you enjoy your favorite drink on your morning break, play a game on your phone over a midday break, and take five minutes at the end of the day to stretch and listen to a favorite song? These things seem small, but unless you schedule them, they will not happen.

- Use a variety of self-care methods. Always choosing to isolate yourself with media or to reward yourself with food or drinks can backfire in the long run. Your small joys need to help you achieve balance and should avoid contributing to social isolation, weight gain, or other problems.

- Be present when you engage in a small joy. If you gobble down your single chocolate while fuming about an interaction with a coworker, you will miss the benefits of your self-care.

Teacher Task #2: Time "Thief"

Your task is to steal back one hour of your life this week . . . in five-minute increments! That makes twelve opportunities this week to take care of yourself.

Make a chart like this one with twelve rows (one for each five-minute increment). Fill out each row to plan what you will do and when you will do it. Once you complete an item, check it off in the "Done!" column to celebrate your success!

WHAT I WILL DO	WHEN I WILL DO IT	DONE!

116

How Can I Help? A Teacher's Guide to Early Childhood Behavioral Health

Appendix A: Blank Release-of-Information Form

_____ (name of child-care center or school)

_____ (street address)

_____ (city, state, ZIP/postal code)

Release-of-Information Form

I, _____ (name of parent/guardian),

parent/guardian of _____ (name of child),

born _____ (child's date of birth), provide my signature

below for written consent for _____
(name of teacher and/or director or principal) of

_____ (name of child-care center or school)
to share and receive information with the following person:

Name and role (pediatrician, counselor, etc.) _____

Address _____

Phone _____

Fax _____

This consent will expire one year from the date listed here or may be withdrawn by the parent/guardian at any time.

_____   _____
Parent/guardian signature   Date

_____   _____
Teacher signature   Date

_____   _____
Director/principal signature   Date

Gryphon House

How Can I Help? A Teacher's Guide to Early Childhood Behavioral Health

Appendix B: Sample Filled-Out Release-of-Information Form

ABC Child-Care Center
123 Main Street
Anytown, USA

Release-of-Information Form

I, Jane Doe, parent/guardian of John Doe, born January 1, 2016, provide my signature below for written consent for Shawna Jones of ABC Child-Care Center to share and receive information with the following person:

Dr. Kenyae Smith, pediatrician
456 Central Rd., Anytown, USA
Phone (555) 123-4567
Fax (555) 765-4321

This consent will expire one year from the date listed here or may be withdrawn by the parent/guardian at any time.

_____   _____
Parent/guardian signature   Date

_____   _____
Teacher signature   Date

_____   _____
Director/principal signature   Date

How Can I Help? A Teacher's Guide to Early Childhood Behavioral Health

References and Recommended Reading

ACES Too High News. n.d. "Got Your ACE Score?" ACES Too High News. https://acestoohigh.com/got-your-ace-score/

Ackerman, Courtney. 2017. "Cognitive Distortions: When Your Brain Lies to You (+ PDF Worksheets)." Positive Psychology Program. https://positivepsychologyprogram.com/cognitive-distortions/

Adam, Emma, Megan Gunnar, and Akiko Tanaka. 2004. "Adult Attachment, Parent Emotion, and Observed Parenting Behavior: Mediator and Moderator Models." *Child Development* 75(1): 110–122.

American Academy of Child and Adolescent Psychiatry. 2018. "Depression Resource Center." American Academy of Child and Adolescent Psychiatry. https://www.aacap.org/aacap/Families_and_Youth/Resource_Centers/Depression_Resource_Center/Home.aspx

American Academy of Child and Adolescent Psychiatry. 2017. "Anxiety and Children." American Academy of Child and Adolescent Psychiatry. https://www.aacap.org/aacap/Families_and_Youth/Facts_for_Families/FFF-Guide/The-Anxious-Child-047.aspx

American Academy of Pediatrics. 2018a. "Healthy Sleep Habits: How Many Hours Does Your Child Need?" Healthychildren.org. https://www.healthychildren.org/English/healthy-living/sleep/Pages/Healthy-Sleep-Habits-How-Many-Hours-Does-Your-Child-Need.aspx

American Academy of Pediatrics. 2018b. "Study Suggests Parents Shouldn't Worry if Their Infant Doesn't Sleep through the Night by Six to Twelve Months of Age." American Academy of Pediatrics. https://www.aap.org/en-us/about-the-aap/aap-press-room/Pages/Parents-Shouldnt-Worry-if-Their-Infant-Doesnt-Sleep-Through-the-Night.aspx

American Psychiatric Association. 2013a. *Diagnostic and Statistical Manual of Mental Disorders.* 5th ed. Washington, DC: American Psychiatric Association Publishing.

American Psychiatric Association. 2013b. *Highlights of Changes from DSM-IV-TR to DSM-5.* Washington, DC: American Psychiatric Association.

American Sleep Association. 2018a. "Night Terrors, Sleep Terrors: Screaming During the Night." American Sleep Association. https://www.sleepassociation.org/sleep-disorders/night-terrors/

American Sleep Association. 2018b. "Sleep Walking: Facts, Causes, Symptoms, and Treatment." American Sleep Association. https://www.sleepassociation.org/sleep-disorders/more-sleep-disorders/sleep-walking/

American Speech-Language-Hearing Association. n.d. "Selective Mutism." American Speech-Language-Hearing Association. https://www.asha.org/public/speech/disorders/selective-mutism/

Breathnach, Sarah. 1995. *Simple Abundance: A Daybook of Comfort and Joy.* New York, NY: Warner Books.

Brenner Children's Hospital. 2012. "Separation Anxiety." Brenner Children's Hospital. https://www.brennerchildrens.org/KidsHealth/Parents/Pregnancy-and-Baby/Communicating-With-Your-Baby/Separation-Anxiety.htm

Bronfenbrenner, Urie. 1979. *The Ecology of Human Development: Experiments by Nature and Design.* Cambridge, MA: Harvard University Press.

Burke, Nadine, et al. 2011. "The Impact of Adverse Childhood Experiences on an Urban Pediatric Population." *Child Abuse and Neglect* 35(6): 408–413.

Center for the Study of Social Policy. 2018. "Strengthening Families: Increasing Positive Outcomes for Children and Families." Center for the Study of Social Policy. https://www.cssp.org/young-children-their-families/strengtheningfamilies/about

Center on the Developing Child at Harvard University. 2018. "Center on the Developing Child at Harvard University" (homepage). Center on the Developing Child at Harvard University. https://developingchild.harvard.edu/

Center on the Developing Child at Harvard University. 2019. "Toxic Stress Derails Healthy Development." Center on the Developing Child at Harvard University. https://developingchild.harvard.edu/resources/toxic-stress-derails-healthy-development/

Centers for Disease Control and Prevention. 2018. "CDC's Developmental Milestones." Centers for Disease Control and Prevention. https://www.cdc.gov/ncbddd/actearly/milestones/index.html

Charach, Alice, et al. 2013. "Interventions for Preschool Children at High Risk for ADHD: A Comparative Effectiveness Review." *Pediatrics* 131(5): e1584–e1604. http://pediatrics.aappublications.org/content/131/5/e1584

122

How Can I Help? A Teacher's Guide to Early Childhood Behavioral Health

Children's Hospital of Philadelphia. 2018. "Developmental Milestones." Children's Hospital of Philadelphia. https://www.chop.edu/conditions-diseases/developmental-milestones

Cohen, Daniel, et al. 2010. "Uncovering Residual Effects of Chronic Sleep Loss on Human Performance." *Science Translational Medicine* 2(14): 14ra3.

Donatelli, Jo-Ann, Jane Bybee, and Stephen Buka. 2007. "What Do Mothers Make Adolescents Feel Guilty About? Incidents, Reactions, and Relation to Depression." *Journal of Child and Family Studies* 16(6): 859–875.

Egger, Helen, and Adrian Angold. 2004. "Stressful Life Events and PTSD in Preschool Children." Paper presented at the Annual Meeting of the American Academy of Child and Adolescent Psychiatry, Washington, DC.

Erikson, Erik. 1986. *Childhood and Society.* 2nd ed. New York, NY: W. W. Norton.

Eriksson, Malin, Mehdi Ghazinour, and Anne Hammarström. 2018. "Different Uses of Bronfenbrenner's Ecological Theory in Public Mental Health Research: What Is Their Value for Guiding Public Mental Health Policy and Practice?" *Social Theory and Health* 16(4): 414–433.

Felitti, Vincent, et al. 1998. "Relationship of Childhood Abuse and Household Dysfunction to Many of the Leading Causes of Death in Adults: The Adverse Childhood Experiences (ACE) Study." *American Journal of Preventive Medicine* 14(4): 245–258.

Grohol, John. 2019. "15 Common Cognitive Distortions." Psych Central. https://psychcentral.com/lib/15-common-cognitive-distortions/

Gross, Gail. 2016. "Three Developmental Charts: Erikson, Kohlberg, and Piaget." *HuffPost*, August 10, https://www.huffingtonpost.com/entry/three-developmental-charts-erikson-kohlberg-and_us_57a6a4b1e4b034b258952178

James, Sarah, et al. 2018. "Association of Preterm Birth with ADHD-Like Cognitive Impairments and Additional Subtle Impairments in Attention and Arousal Malleability." *Psychological Medicine* 48(9): 1484–1493.

Johns Hopkins Medicine. n.d. "Toilet Training." Johns Hopkins Medicine. https://www.hopkinsmedicine.org/healthlibrary/conditions/pediatrics/toilet-training_90,P02300

Joinson, Carol, et al. 2018. "A Prospective Cohort Study of Biopsychosocial Factors Associated with Childhood Urinary Incontinence." *European Child and Adolescent Psychiatry* 27: 1–8. https://doi.org/10.1007/s00787-018-1193-1

Joseph, Stephen. 2012. "Unconditional Positive Regard." Psychology Today. https://www.psychologytoday.com/us/blog/what-doesnt-kill-us/201210/unconditional-positive-regard

Kihlstrom, John. 1996. "The Trauma-Memory Argument and Recovered Memory Therapy." In *The Recovered Memory/False Memory Debate*. San Diego, CA: Academic Press.

Lewin, Daniel, and Edward Huntley. 2010. "Behavioral Insomnias of Childhood: Assessment and Treatment." In *Clinical Handbook of Insomnia*. Totowa, NJ: Humana Press.

Luby, Joan. 2009. "Early Childhood Depression." *The American Journal of Psychiatry* 166(9): 974–979.

McAdam, David, et al. 2004. "Behavioral Interventions to Reduce the Pica of Persons with Developmental Disabilities." *Behavior Modification* 28(1): 45–72.

Mian, Nicholas, et al. 2011. "An Ecological Risk Model for Early Childhood Anxiety: The Importance of Early Child Symptoms and Temperament." *Journal of Abnormal Child Psychology* 39(4): 501–512.

Morley, Tara, and Greg Moran. 2011. "The Origins of Cognitive Vulnerability in Early Childhood: Mechanisms Linking Early Attachment to Later Depression." *Clinical Psychology Review* 31(7): 1071–1082.

Murphy, Anne, et al. 2014. "Adverse Childhood Experiences (ACEs) Questionnaire and Adult Attachment Interview (AAI): Implications for Parent-Child Relationships." *Child Abuse and Neglect* 38(2): 224–233.

Nachmias, Melissa, et al. 1996. "Behavioral Inhibition and Stress Reactivity: The Moderating Role of Attachment Security." *Child Development* 67(2): 508–522.

National Eating Disorders Association. 2018. "Information by Eating Disorder." National Eating Disorders Association. https://www.nationaleatingdisorders.org/information-eating-disorder

National Education Association. 2006. *The Twice-Exceptional Dilemma*. Washington, DC: National Education Association. http://www.nea.org/assets/docs/twiceexceptional.pdf

National Scientific Council on the Developing Child. 2014. "Excessive Stress Disrupts the Architecture of the Developing Brain." Updated ed. Working Paper 3, Harvard University, Cambridge, MA. https://developingchild.harvard.edu/wp-content/uploads/2005/05/Stress_Disrupts_Architecture_Developing_Brain-1.pdf

124

How Can I Help? A Teacher's Guide to Early Childhood Behavioral Health

Nguyen, Bich Hong, et al. 2008. "Sleep Terrors in Children: A Prospective Study of Twins." *Pediatrics* 122(6): e1164–e1167.

Parritz, Robin, and Michael Troy. 2018. *Disorders of Childhood: Development and Psychopathology.* 3rd ed. Boston, MA: Cengage Learning.

The Pennsylvania Child Welfare Resource Center. n.d. "Thinking about Thinking." The Pennsylvania Child Welfare Resource Center. http://www.pacwrc.pitt. edu/curriculum/313_MngngImpctTrmtcStrssChldWlfrPrfssnl/hndts/HO15_ ThnkngAbtThnkng.pdf

Raising Children Network (Australia). 2019. "Your Premature Baby's Body Language." Raising Children Network (Australia). https://raisingchildren.net.au/newborns/ premature-babies/connecting-communicating/premature-body-language

Rakow, Aaron, et al. 2009. "The Relation of Parental Guilt Induction to Child Internalizing Problems When a Caregiver Has a History of Depression." *Journal of Child and Family Studies* 18(4): 367–377.

Redford, James, dir. 2016. *Resilience: The Biology of Stress and the Science of Hope.* Branford, CT: KPJR Films.

Sheftall, Arielle, et al. 2016. "Suicide in Elementary School-Aged Children and Early Adolescents." *Pediatrics* 138(4): e20160436. http://pediatrics.aappublications.org/ content/138/4/e20160436

Stanford Children's Health. 2018. "Infant Sleep." Stanford Children's Health. https://www.stanfordchildrens.org/en/topic/default?id=infant-sleep-90-P02237

Van der Kolk, Bessel. 2015. *The Body Keeps the Score: Brain, Mind, and Body in the Healing of Trauma.* New York, NY: Penguin Books.

Zero to Three. 2016. *DC:0–5: Diagnostic Classification of Mental Health and Developmental Disorders of Infancy and Early Childhood.* Washington, DC: Zero to Three.

Zero to Three. 2018a. "Infant and Early Childhood Mental Health." Zero to Three. https:// www.zerotothree.org/espanol/infant-and-early-childhood-mental-health

Zero to Three. 2018b. "Your Child's Development: Age-Based Tips from Birth to 36 Months." Zero to Three. https://www.zerotothree.org/resources/series/your-child-s- development-age-based-tips-from-birth-to-36-months

Index

126

How Can I Help? A Teacher's Guide to Early Childhood Behavioral Health

for attention deficit hyperactivity disorder (ADHD), 75–76

for autism spectrum disorder (ASD), 74

for avoidant restrictive food intake disorder (ARFID), 60

for children with difficulty being soothed, 35, 37

for clinginess, 38, 40

for crying, 35, 37, 39

for developmental delays, 35, 37

for disinhibited social engagement disorder (DSED), 29–30

for disorders of sleeping, 64–66

for disorders of toileting, 61–62

for disruptive mood regulation disorder (DMRD), 52–53

for emotional regulation, 39

for excessive separation problems or separation anxiety disorder, 36, 38, 40, 46–47

for generalized anxiety disorder (GAD), 49

for global developmental delay (GDD), 72–73

for infants and young children who have experienced trauma, 35–41

for intellectual disability (ID) or intellectual developmental disorder (IDD), 71–72

for lack of social interest, 36, 38, 40

for learning problems, 39

for major depressive disorder (MDD), 53–54

for pica, 58

for poor physical growth, 35, 37

for poor sleep quality or daytime sleepiness, 35, 37, 39

for reactive attachment disorder (RAD), 28

for rumination disorder, 59

for selective mutism, 48

for sexual-behavior problems, 38, 41

for withdrawal, 36, 38, 40

M ••••••••••••••••••••••••••

Major depressive disorder (MDD), 103

Mental health

biological factors and, 1–4

diagnostic sources, 16–17

environmental factors and, 5–8

prevention efforts, 13–16

relational factors and, 8–10

vocabulary, 17–18

working with family members with disorders, 97–104

Mental-health providers, 86–89

child-development specialists, 82, 88

child-guidance specialists, 82

counselors, 86–87

infant-mental-health (IMH) specialists, 15, 17, 86, 88–89

occupational therapists (OTs), 15, 64, 74, 89

physical therapists (PTs), 89

psychiatrists, child, 86

psychologists, 15, 82, 86–87

social workers, 87–88

speech-language pathologists (SLPs), 15, 89

Modeling, 9–10, 34, 37, 52–54, 60

Mood disorders

anxiety disorders in adults, 102–103

Release-of-information forms, 28–29, 31, 34, 37–38, 41, 48, 54, 59–60, 64, 75, 81, 117–119

Routines

maintaining predictable, 28, 46, 49, 74–76

sleep, 62–64, 67

Rumination disorder, 58–59

S

Selective mutism, 47–48

Self-care, teacher's, 107–116

Sensory difficulties, 71–74

Sensory vocabulary, 17–18

Sleep, disorders of, 62–66. *See also* Parasomnias

Social and cognitive development, Erikson's theory of, 8–10

Social anxiety disorder, 102–103

Social skills, opportunities for child to practice, 37

Suicide, 54

T

Teachers. *See also* Intervention strategies

communication with families. *See* Communication with family members

reporting suspected child maltreatment, 28, 104

role in prevention, 13–16

role in referral and assessment processes, 79

stress-management techniques for, 110–111

Teacher tasks

adjusting vocabulary for talking to children, 54–55

describing a child for a referral, 82–83

determining ACE score, 25

exploring children's ecological systems, 8

exploring executive functioning, 69–70

finding simple joys, 114–116

planning for difficult conversations, 96–97

planning for prevention, 15–16

situational anxiety, 49–51

sleep calculations, 63

Therapy, 86–87

Toileting, disorders of, 60–62

Trauma, 23–24

care and guidance strategies for children exposed to, 34–41

disorders related to, 27–34

possible symptoms of exposure to, 25–26